The Path To Success

Dr. Kumar Abhisek

Published by Dr. Kumar Abhisek, 2024.

While every precaution has been taken in the preparation of this book, the publisher assumes no responsibility for errors or omissions, or for damages resulting from the use of the information contained herein.

THE PATH TO SUCCESS

Table of Contents

To my family,Thank you for your unwavering support, love, and patience throughout this journey.Your belief in me has been my greatest source of strength.

To my mentors,for your wisdom, guidance, and inspiration, which have shaped my path and fueled my ambition.

And to every reader,who dares to dream and strives to achieve—this book is for you. May it serve as a beacon of hope and a tool for your growth.

The Path to Success

Principles for Personal and Professional Growth

Dr. Kumar Abhisek

Chapter 1: Take 100% Responsibility for Your Life

Overview

Taking full responsibility for your life means acknowledging that you are in control of your destiny. It involves understanding that your choices and actions determine your outcomes. When you take responsibility for your life, you move away from the habit of blaming others or external circumstances for your failures and challenges. Instead, you recognize your power to make different choices and take proactive steps toward your goals. This mindset shift is crucial for achieving lasting success, as it empowers you to create the life you desire.

Real-Life Examples

Oprah Winfrey

Oprah Winfrey is a prime example of someone who has taken full responsibility for her life. Born into poverty in rural Mississippi, Oprah faced numerous challenges, including a difficult family environment and experiences of abuse. Despite these hardships, she decided early on to take control of her life and not let her circumstances define her.

Oprah excelled in school and pursued higher education, eventually landing a job in radio while still in high school. Her career in media took off, leading her to become a successful talk show host, producer, and philanthropist. Oprah's ability to take responsibility for her choices and actions, rather than blaming her difficult past, enabled her to build a media empire and inspire millions of people worldwide.

J.K. Rowling

J.K. Rowling's journey to success is another powerful example of taking responsibility for one's life. Before the phenomenal success of the Harry Potter series, Rowling faced numerous rejections and personal struggles. She was a single mother living on welfare, struggling to make ends meet while writing her first book.

Despite these challenges, Rowling took responsibility for her dream of becoming a writer. She continued to write and revise her manuscript, submitting it to multiple publishers until it was finally accepted. Her perseverance and refusal to blame external circumstances for her difficulties led to the creation of one of the most beloved and successful book series in history.

Tips

Eliminate Blame and Excuses

One of the first steps to taking full responsibility for your life is to eliminate blame and excuses from your vocabulary. When you blame others or external factors for your problems, you give away your power to change the situation. Instead, acknowledge your role in creating or perpetuating the issue, and focus on what you can do to address it.

For example, if you are unhappy in your job, instead of blaming your boss or coworkers, consider what actions you can take to improve your situation. Could you improve your skills, seek a transfer to a different department, or even look for a new job? By taking responsibility for your circumstances, you empower yourself to make positive changes.

Recognize Your Power to Change Your Circumstances

Recognizing your power to change your circumstances is essential for taking responsibility for your life. Understand that while you may not be able to control everything that happens to you, you can always control your response and actions.

For instance, if you face a setback, such as a failed business venture or a personal loss, focus on what you can learn from the experience and how you can move forward. By adopting a proactive mindset, you can turn challenges into opportunities for growth and improvement.

Exercises

Responsibility Audit

A Responsibility Audit is a powerful exercise to help you identify areas in your life where you may be blaming others or external circumstances. Take some time to reflect on different aspects of your life, such as your career, relationships, health, and personal goals. For each area, ask yourself the following questions:

Are there any situations where I am blaming others for my problems?

What excuses am I making that prevent me from taking action?

How can I take responsibility for my current circumstances?

Write down your answers and identify specific actions you can take to assume responsibility for each area. This exercise will help you become more aware of your thoughts and behaviours, and encourage you to take proactive steps toward achieving your goals.

Daily Reflection

Daily reflection is another effective exercise to help you take responsibility for your life. At the end of each day, take a few minutes to reflect on your actions and decisions. Ask yourself the following questions:

Did I take responsibility for my choices and actions today?

Were there any situations where I blamed others or made excuses?

How could I have handled those situations differently?

What can I do tomorrow to take more responsibility for my life?

By incorporating daily reflection into your routine, you can continuously improve your mindset and behaviour, making it easier to take responsibility for your life.

Inspirational Quotes

Inspirational quotes can serve as powerful reminders of the importance of taking responsibility for your life. Here are a few quotes to inspire you:

"You must take personal responsibility. You cannot change the circumstances, the seasons, or the wind, but you can change yourself." – Jim Rohn

"The moment you take responsibility for everything in your life is the moment you can change anything in your life." – Hal Elrod

"Responsibility is the price of freedom." – Elbert Hubbard

"In the final analysis, the one quality that all successful people have is the ability to take on responsibility." – Michael Korda

Understanding Responsibility

Taking responsibility for your life is about understanding that you are the architect of your own destiny. It means acknowledging that your thoughts, actions, and decisions shape your reality. By taking responsibility, you empower yourself to create the life you want, rather than being a passive victim of circumstances.

The Victim Mentality

A victim mentality is characterized by blaming others for your problems and feeling powerless to change your situation. This mindset can be detrimental to your success and well-being, as it prevents you from taking proactive steps to improve your life.

Signs of a victim mentality include:

Blaming others for your failures or difficulties

Making excuses for why you can't achieve your goals

Feeling powerless to change your circumstances

Focusing on negative aspects of your life rather than seeking solutions

To overcome a victim mentality, you need to shift your mindset and take responsibility for your life. This involves recognizing that you have the power to make different choices and take action to create the life you desire.

Embracing Responsibility

Embracing responsibility means accepting that you are in control of your life and taking ownership of your actions and decisions. It involves a commitment to self-improvement and a willingness to learn from your mistakes.

Here are some steps to help you embrace responsibility:

Acknowledge Your Role: Recognize that you are responsible for your thoughts, actions, and decisions. Accept that your current circumstances are a result of your past choices.

Focus on Solutions: Instead of dwelling on problems or blaming others, focus on finding solutions. Ask yourself what you can do to improve the situation.

Take Action: Take proactive steps to achieve your goals and address challenges. Break down your goals into manageable tasks and take consistent action.

Learn from Mistakes: View mistakes and setbacks as opportunities for growth. Reflect on what you can learn from each experience and how you can improve in the future.

Seek Feedback: Be open to feedback from others and use it to improve yourself. Constructive criticism can help you identify areas for growth and development.

The Benefits of Taking Responsibility

Taking responsibility for your life offers numerous benefits, including:

Empowerment: When you take responsibility, you empower yourself to create the life you want. You realize that you have the power to make different choices and take action to achieve your goals.

Personal Growth: Taking responsibility encourages self-reflection and continuous improvement. By learning from your mistakes and seeking feedback, you can grow and develop as a person.

Improved Relationships: When you take responsibility for your actions, you build trust and credibility with others. This can lead to stronger and more positive relationships.

Greater Success: Taking responsibility for your life increases your chances of success. By focusing on solutions and taking action, you are more likely to achieve your goals and overcome challenges.

Overcoming Common Obstacles

Taking responsibility for your life is not always easy, and you may encounter obstacles along the way. Here are some common challenges and how to overcome them:

Fear of Failure: The fear of failure can prevent you from taking responsibility for your life. To overcome this fear, reframe failure as a learning opportunity. Understand that mistakes are a natural part of the growth process and can provide valuable lessons.

Lack of Confidence: A lack of confidence can make it difficult to take responsibility for your life. Build your confidence by setting small, achievable goals and celebrating your successes. Surround yourself with supportive people who encourage and uplift you.

Negative Influences: Negative influences, such as toxic relationships or unsupportive environments, can hinder your ability to take responsibility for your life. Identify and minimize contact with negative influences, and seek out positive and supportive relationships.

Procrastination: Procrastination can prevent you from taking action and achieving your goals. Combat procrastination by breaking tasks into smaller, manageable steps and setting deadlines for yourself. Use tools such as to-do lists and calendars to stay organized and focused.

Developing a Responsibility Mindset

Developing a responsibility mindset involves cultivating habits and attitudes that support taking responsibility for your life. Here are some tips to help you develop this mindset:

Practice Self-Awareness: Regularly reflect on your thoughts, actions, and decisions. Identify areas where you can take more responsibility and make improvements.

Set Clear Goals: Set clear, specific goals for yourself and take consistent action to achieve them. Break down your goals into manageable steps and track your progress.

Cultivate Resilience: Develop resilience by learning to bounce back from setbacks and challenges. View difficulties as opportunities for growth and focus on finding solutions.

Stay Accountable: Hold yourself accountable for your actions and decisions. Set up accountability systems, such as sharing your goals with a trusted friend or mentor, to help you stay on track.

Maintain a Positive Attitude: Adopt a positive attitude and focus on what you

can control. Practice gratitude and positive thinking to reinforce a responsibility mindset.

Implementing Responsibility in Different Areas of Life

Taking responsibility for your life should extend to various areas, including your career, relationships, health, and personal development. Here's how you can apply responsibility principles in each area:

Career

Set Career Goals: Define what you want to achieve in your career and create a plan to reach those goals. This might include acquiring new skills, seeking promotions, or changing careers.

Seek Feedback: Regularly ask for feedback from supervisors and colleagues to identify areas for improvement. Use this feedback to enhance your performance and professional growth.

Take Initiative: Don't wait for opportunities to come to you. Proactively seek out projects, volunteer for challenging tasks, and demonstrate leadership.

Relationships

Communicate Openly: Take responsibility for your communication in relationships. Express your thoughts and feelings clearly and listen actively to others.

Resolve Conflicts: When conflicts arise, take responsibility for your role in the situation. Approach conflicts with a problem-solving mindset and seek mutually beneficial solutions.

Support Others: Be accountable for your actions in supporting friends, family, and colleagues. Show up for others, keep your commitments, and offer help when needed.

Health

Adopt Healthy Habits: Take responsibility for your physical health by adopting healthy habits such as regular exercise, balanced nutrition, and adequate sleep.

Seek Medical Advice: Don't ignore health issues or delay seeking medical advice. Take proactive steps to maintain your health and well-being.

Manage Stress: Develop strategies for managing stress, such as mindfulness, meditation, or hobbies that help you relax and recharge.

Personal Development

Set Personal Goals: Define what personal growth means to you and set goals to achieve it. This could include learning new skills, pursuing hobbies, or improving your emotional intelligence.

Reflect and Learn: Regularly reflect on your experiences and learn from them. Identify lessons learned and apply them to future situations.

Embrace Lifelong Learning: Take responsibility for your ongoing education and development. Read books, take courses, and seek new experiences to expand your knowledge and skills.

Case Studies of Responsibility

To further illustrate the importance of taking responsibility, let's explore two detailed case studies:

Case Study 1: Elon Musk

Elon Musk, the CEO of SpaceX and Tesla, exemplifies taking responsibility for one's vision and goals. Musk faced numerous challenges and setbacks on his path to success, from nearly going bankrupt to facing scepticism and criticism from the public and industry experts.

Instead of blaming external circumstances, Musk took full responsibility for his vision. He invested his own money into his companies, worked tirelessly to solve technical problems, and continued to push forward despite failures. His ability to take responsibility for his ambitions has led to groundbreaking achievements in electric vehicles, space exploration, and renewable energy.

Case Study 2: Sheryl Sandberg

Sheryl Sandberg, the COO of Facebook and author of "Lean In," has shown remarkable responsibility in her professional and personal life. After the sudden death of her husband, Sandberg faced immense personal grief while continuing to lead at Facebook.

Rather than letting her circumstances overwhelm her, Sandberg took responsibility for her emotional well-being and her role at work. She sought therapy, leaned on her support network, and continued to advocate for women in the workplace. Her journey of resilience and responsibility has inspired many to take control of their lives and careers.

Creating a Responsibility Action Plan

To help you implement the principles of responsibility in your life, create a Responsibility Action Plan. This plan should outline specific steps you will take to embrace responsibility in different areas of your life.

Steps to Create Your Responsibility Action Plan:

Identify Areas for Improvement: Reflect on areas of your life where you need to take more responsibility. These could include your career, relationships, health, or personal development.

Set Clear Goals: Define clear, actionable goals for each area. Ensure these goals are specific, measurable, achievable, relevant, and time-bound (SMART).

Develop Action Steps: Break down each goal into smaller, manageable action steps. Outline what you will do daily, weekly, and monthly to achieve your goals.

Seek Support: Identify individuals who can support you in your journey. This could include friends, family, mentors, or professional coaches.

Track Your Progress: Regularly review your progress and make adjustments as needed. Celebrate your successes and learn from any setbacks.

Example of a Responsibility Action Plan:

Area: Career

Goal: Secure a promotion to a managerial position within the next 12 months.

Action Steps:

Daily: Dedicate at least one hour to professional development through reading, online courses, or webinars.

Weekly: Seek feedback from supervisors and colleagues to identify areas for improvement.

Monthly: Network with professionals in your industry and attend relevant events or conferences.

Support: Find a mentor within your organization to provide guidance and advice.

Tracking: Keep a journal of your daily activities, feedback received, and progress toward your goal. Review this journal monthly and adjust your action steps as needed.

Conclusion

Taking 100% responsibility for your life is a transformative principle that empowers you to create the life you desire. By eliminating blame and excuses, recognizing your power to change your circumstances, and taking proactive steps toward your goals, you can achieve greater success and fulfilment.

Remember, taking responsibility is a continuous process. It requires self-awareness, a commitment to growth, and a willingness to learn from your experiences. As you embrace responsibility in all areas of your life, you will develop the confidence and resilience needed to overcome challenges and achieve your dreams.

Inspirational Quotes to Keep You Motivated:

"The price of greatness is responsibility." – Winston Churchill

"It is not what happens to you, but how you respond to it that matters." – Epictetus

"Act as if what you do makes a difference. It does." – William James

"If you own this story you get to write the ending." – Brené Brown

By incorporating these principles and practices into your daily life, you can take full responsibility for your journey and unlock your true potential.

Chapter 2: Define Your Purpose and Vision

Overview

Having a clear purpose and vision acts as a guiding star for your life, helping you stay focused and motivated. Your purpose is the fundamental reason for your existence, while your vision is a vivid description of what you want your life to look like in the future. Together, they provide direction, meaning, and inspiration, ensuring that you remain committed to your goals even in the face of challenges. By defining your purpose and vision, you align your daily actions with your long-term aspirations, leading to a more fulfilling and successful life.

Real-Life Examples

Steve Jobs

Steve Jobs, the co-founder of Apple, had a clear vision that transformed not only his company but also the technology industry as a whole. Jobs envisioned creating products that were not only functional but also beautiful and user-friendly. This vision drove Apple's innovation and success, resulting in groundbreaking products such as the iPod, iPhone, and iPad.

Jobs' unwavering commitment to his vision inspired his team to push the boundaries of what was possible. His ability to articulate and pursue a clear vision allowed Apple to become one of the most valuable and influential companies in the world. Jobs' story illustrates the power of having a clear vision and the impact it can have on both personal and professional success.

Nelson Mandela

Nelson Mandela's vision of a free and democratic South Africa sustained him through 27 years of imprisonment and numerous challenges. Mandela's purpose was to end apartheid and establish a society based on equality and justice. Despite the immense personal sacrifices he endured, Mandela remained steadfast in his vision.

Mandela's ability to maintain his vision during his imprisonment and throughout his political career inspired millions of people worldwide. His leadership and commitment to his purpose ultimately led to the dismantling of apartheid and the establishment of a democratic South Africa. Mandela's story exemplifies the importance of having a clear vision and purpose, especially in the face of adversity.

Tips

Write a Personal Vision Statement

A personal vision statement is a concise declaration of what you want to achieve in your life. It should reflect your core values, aspirations, and long-term goals. Writing a personal vision statement helps you clarify your purpose and provides a roadmap for your future.

To create your personal vision statement, consider the following steps:

Reflect on Your Values: Identify your core values and what matters most to you. These values will form the foundation of your vision statement.

Visualize Your Ideal Future: Imagine your life five, ten, or twenty years from now. Consider your career, relationships, health, and personal growth. What do you want to achieve in each area?

Write Your Vision Statement: Combine your values and aspirations into a clear and concise statement. Ensure that it is inspiring and resonates with you on a deep level.

Review and Refine: Revisit your vision statement regularly and make adjustments as needed. As you grow and evolve, your vision may change, and it's important to keep it aligned with your current goals and values.

Reflect on What Excites and Fulfils You

To define your purpose and vision, it's essential to reflect on what excites and fulfils you. Consider the activities, experiences, and goals that bring you joy and satisfaction. By understanding what truly excites you, you can align your vision with your passions and create a more meaningful and fulfilling life.

Here are some questions to help you reflect on what excites and fulfils you:

What Activities Bring You Joy? Think about the activities you love doing, whether it's a hobby, a type of work, or spending time with certain people.

What Are Your Passions? Identify the subjects or causes you are passionate about. What topics do you love learning about, and what issues do you feel strongly about?

What Are Your Strengths? Reflect on your natural talents and strengths. What are you good at, and what do others often seek your help with?

What Achievements Make You Proud? Consider the accomplishments in your life that you are most proud of.

Reflect on the process of achieving those accomplishments and why they are significant to you.

By answering these questions, you can gain insights into what excites and fulfils you, helping you to define a purpose and vision that align with your passions and strengths.

Exercises

Vision Board

Creating a vision board is a powerful exercise that helps you visualize your goals and dreams. A vision board is a collage of images, words, and quotes that represent what you want to achieve in your life. By placing it in a location where you see it regularly, a vision board serves as a constant reminder of your aspirations and motivates you to take action.

Steps to Create a Vision Board:

Gather Supplies: You will need a board (corkboard, poster board, or a large piece of paper), magazines, scissors, glue, and markers.

Reflect on Your Goals: Spend some time thinking about your long-term and short-term goals in different areas of your life, such as career, health, relationships, and personal growth.

Find Inspirational Images and Words: Look through magazines or print images from the internet that represent your goals and dreams. Choose pictures, words, and quotes that resonate with you.

Arrange and Glue: Arrange the images and words on your board in a way that feels meaningful and inspiring to you. Once you're happy with the layout, glue everything in place.

Display Your Vision Board: Place your vision board in a prominent location where you will see it daily. This could be your bedroom, office, or any other space where you spend a lot of time.

Purpose Journal

Writing in a purpose journal is another effective exercise to help you clarify your purpose. This exercise involves regularly writing about your passions, strengths, values, and goals. By journaling, you can gain deeper insights into what drives you and how you can align your actions with your purpose.

Steps to Start a Purpose Journal:

Choose a Journal: Select a notebook or digital app that you will use exclusively for your purpose journal.

Set Aside Time: Dedicate a specific time each day or week to write in your journal. Consistency is key to gaining the most benefit from this exercise.

Reflect on Key Questions: Use prompts to guide your journaling. Some questions to consider include:

What are my core values?

What activities make me feel most alive and fulfilled?

What are my greatest strengths and talents?

What impact do I want to have on the world?

What are my long-term and short-term goals?

Review and Reflect: Periodically review your journal entries to identify patterns and themes. Use these insights to refine your purpose and vision.

Inspirational Quotes

Inspirational quotes can serve as powerful reminders of the importance of having a clear purpose and vision. Here are some quotes to inspire you:

"The two most important days in your life are the day you are born and the day you find out why." – Mark Twain

"Efforts and courage are not enough without purpose and direction." – John F. Kennedy

"Your purpose in life is to find your purpose and give your whole heart and soul to it." – Buddha

"When you have a clear purpose, you won't have time for negativity." – Mark Victor Hansen

The Importance of Purpose and Vision

Defining your purpose and vision is crucial for several reasons:

Provides Direction: A clear purpose and vision act as a compass, guiding your decisions and actions. They help you stay focused on what truly matters and avoid distractions.

Increases Motivation: Knowing your purpose and having a vision for your future provides intrinsic motivation. It gives you a reason to push through challenges and stay committed to your goals.

Enhances Resilience: When you have a strong sense of purpose, you are more likely to persevere in the face of adversity. Your vision serves as a reminder of why you started and what you are working towards.

Fosters Fulfilment: Living a purpose-driven life leads to greater fulfilment and satisfaction. When your actions align with your values and passions, you experience a deeper sense of meaning.

Developing Your Purpose and Vision

Developing a clear purpose and vision involves introspection and self-awareness. It requires you to dig deep and understand what truly matters to you. Here are some steps to help you develop your purpose and vision:

1. Reflect on Your Values

Your values are the principles that guide your behaviour and decisions. They are deeply rooted in what you believe is important. To identify your values, consider the following questions:

What principles do I hold dear?

What beliefs guide my actions and decisions?

What values do I want to embody in my daily life?

2. Identify Your Passions

Your passions are the activities and subjects that excite and energize you. They are often indicators of your purpose. To identify your passions, ask yourself:

What activities make me lose track of time?

What topics do I love learning about?

What causes do I feel strongly about?

3. Recognize Your Strengths

Your strengths are your natural talents and abilities. They are the things you do well and enjoy doing. To identify your strengths, consider:

What tasks do I excel at?

What skills do others frequently praise me for?

What activities come naturally to me?

4. Envision Your Ideal Future

Take some time to visualize your ideal future. Imagine where you want to be in five, ten, or twenty years. Consider all aspects of your life, including your career, relationships, health, and personal growth. Ask yourself:

What do I want to achieve in my career?

What kind of relationships do I want to have?

How do I want to take care of my health and well-being?

What personal goals do I want to accomplish?

5. Write Your Vision Statement

Combine your values, passions, strengths, and ideal future into a clear and concise vision statement. Your vision statement should be inspiring and reflect your long-term aspirations. Here's an example of a vision statement:

"My vision is to lead a fulfilling life by using my strengths and passions to make a positive impact on the world. I aspire to build a successful career that aligns with my values, nurture meaningful relationships, and continuously grow and learn."

6. Set Goals Aligned with Your Vision

Once you have a clear vision, set specific goals that align with it. These goals will serve as milestones on your journey toward your vision. Ensure that your goals are SMART: Specific, Measurable, Achievable, Relevant, and Time-bound.

7. Create an Action Plan

Develop an action plan to achieve your goals. Break down your goals into smaller, manageable steps and create a timeline for completing them. Regularly review and adjust your action plan as needed to stay on track.

Living Your Purpose and Vision

Living your purpose and vision involves consistently aligning your actions with your values and goals. It requires dedication, commitment, and a willingness to make adjustments along the way. Here are some tips to help you live your purpose and vision:

Stay Focused

Keep your vision and purpose at the forefront of your mind. Use tools such as vision boards, journals, and reminders to stay focused on what matters most. Avoid distractions and prioritize activities that align with your goals.

Be Adaptable

Life is unpredictable, and circumstances may change. Be adaptable and willing to adjust your vision and goals as needed. Stay open to new opportunities and be flexible in your approach.

Seek Support

Surround yourself with supportive people who encourage and inspire you. Seek out mentors, coaches, and like-minded individuals who can provide guidance and accountability. Share your vision with others and seek their support in achieving it.

Celebrate Progress

Celebrate your achievements and progress along the way. Recognize the small victories and milestones that bring you closer to your vision. Celebrating progress helps to maintain motivation and reinforces your commitment to your goals.

Practice Self-Care

Taking care of your physical, emotional, and mental well-being is essential for living your purpose and vision. Prioritize self-care activities such as exercise, healthy eating, relaxation, and hobbies that bring you joy. Maintaining balance and well-being ensures that you have the energy and resilience to pursue your goals.

Conclusion

Defining your purpose and vision is a transformative process that provides direction, motivation, and fulfilment. By understanding your values, passions, and strengths, you can create a clear vision for your future and set goals that align with it. Living a purpose-driven life requires dedication, adaptability, and support, but the rewards are immense.

Remember, your purpose and vision are unique to you. Take the time to reflect on what truly matters to you and create a vision that inspires and motivates you. As you pursue your purpose and vision, you will experience greater fulfilment and success in all areas of your life.

Inspirational Quotes to Keep You Motivated:

"The two most important days in your life are the day you are born and the day you find out why." – Mark Twain

"Efforts and courage are not enough without purpose and direction." – John F. Kennedy

"Your purpose in life is to find your purpose and give your whole heart and soul to it." – Buddha

"When you have a clear purpose, you won't have time for negativity." – Mark Victor Hansen

By defining your purpose and vision and taking consistent action toward your goals, you can create a life that is meaningful, fulfilling, and aligned with your true self. Embrace the journey and trust in your ability to achieve great things.

Chapter 3: Set Clear, Specific Goals

Overview

Setting clear, specific goals is crucial for achieving success in any area of your life. Goals provide direction, focus, and motivation, helping you to channel your efforts towards meaningful achievements. One of the most effective ways to set goals is by using the SMART criteria, which stands for Specific, Measurable, Achievable, Relevant, and Time-bound. This method ensures that your goals are well-defined and attainable, allowing you to create a structured plan to reach them.

Understanding the importance of setting SMART goals and learning how to break down large goals into manageable steps can make a significant difference in your ability to achieve your aspirations. This chapter will provide real-life examples of individuals who set clear goals and achieved them through persistence, offer tips for effective goal-setting, and guide you through exercises to help you create and achieve your goals.

Real-Life Examples

1. Jim Carrey:

Before Jim Carrey became a household name, he was a struggling actor trying to make it in Hollywood. To motivate himself and maintain a positive outlook, Carrey set a specific, ambitious goal. In 1990, he wrote himself a check for $10 million for "acting services rendered" and dated it for Thanksgiving 1995. He kept the check in his wallet as a constant reminder of his goal.

Carrey worked tirelessly, taking on various roles and honing his craft. By 1994, he had landed leading roles in major films such as "Ace Ventura: Pet Detective," "The Mask," and "Dumb and Dumber," which propelled him to stardom. By Thanksgiving 1995, Carrey had indeed earned $10 million for his role in the movie "Dumb and Dumber." His story illustrates the power of setting clear, specific goals and the determination to achieve them.

2. Serena Williams:

Serena Williams, one of the greatest tennis players of all time, has always been known for her goal-oriented mindset. From a young age, she set specific goals for her career, including winning Grand Slam titles and becoming the world number one. Williams and her coach, who is also her father, Richard Williams, created a detailed plan that included rigorous training, mental conditioning, and strategic match play.

Serena's dedication to her goals paid off. She has won 23 Grand Slam singles titles, four Olympic gold medals, and has held the world number one ranking multiple times. Her ability to set clear, specific goals and follow a structured plan has been a key factor in her success.

3. Elon Musk:

Elon Musk, the founder of SpaceX and CEO of Tesla, is known for his ambitious and specific goals. Musk's vision includes making space travel more affordable and eventually colonizing Mars, as well as accelerating the world's transition to sustainable energy. To achieve these goals, Musk has set numerous specific objectives for his companies.

For example, with SpaceX, Musk set the goal of developing a reusable rocket, which would significantly reduce the cost of space travel. Despite numerous failures and setbacks, SpaceX successfully launched and landed the first reusable rocket in 2015. Musk's commitment to clear, specific goals and his persistence in achieving them have revolutionized the aerospace and automotive industries.

Tips for Setting Clear, Specific Goals

1. Write Down Your Goals:

Writing down your goals is a powerful way to solidify your intentions and increase your commitment to achieving them. When you put your goals in writing, you create a tangible record that you can refer to and review regularly. This practice helps to keep your goals at the forefront of your mind and reinforces your dedication to achieving them.

2. Use the SMART Criteria:

Ensure that your goals are Specific, Measurable, Achievable, Relevant, and Time-bound. This method provides a clear framework for setting effective goals that are realistic and attainable.

Specific: Clearly define what you want to achieve. The more specific your goal, the easier it will be to create a plan to achieve it.

Measurable: Establish criteria for measuring your progress. This allows you to track your progress and stay motivated.

Achievable: Set goals that are challenging but attainable. Consider your resources and constraints when setting your goals.

Relevant: Ensure that your goals align with your values, long-term objectives, and priorities. Your goals should be meaningful and significant to you.

Time-bound: Set a deadline for achieving your goals. Having a timeframe creates a sense of urgency and helps you stay focused.

3. Break Down Large Goals into Manageable Steps:

Large goals can often feel overwhelming. Breaking them down into smaller, manageable steps makes them more achievable and less daunting. Create a step-by-step action plan that outlines the specific tasks you need to complete to reach your goal. Focus on completing one step at a time, and celebrate your progress along the way.

4. Review and Adjust Your Goals Regularly:

Regularly reviewing your goals allows you to track your progress, make adjustments, and stay on course. Life is dynamic, and your goals may need to be modified as circumstances change. Set aside time to review your goals periodically, reflect on your progress, and make any necessary adjustments to keep moving forward.

5. Stay Committed and Persistent:

Achieving your goals requires commitment and persistence. Stay focused on your objectives, even when you encounter obstacles or setbacks. Remind yourself of the reasons why you set your goals in the first place and keep pushing forward. Persistence and determination are key to overcoming challenges and achieving success.

Exercises

1. Create a List of Short-Term and Long-Term Goals:

Take some time to create a list of your short-term and long-term goals. Short-term goals are objectives that you aim to achieve within the next few months to a year, while long-term goals are those that you plan to achieve over several years.

Steps to Create Your List:

Reflect on Different Areas of Your Life: Consider your career, relationships, health, personal growth, finances, and other important areas. What do you want to achieve in each area?

Be Specific: Write down your goals in clear, specific terms. Avoid vague statements and ensure that each goal is well-defined.

Prioritize Your Goals: Rank your goals in order of importance. Focus on the goals that are most meaningful and significant to you.

Example of a List of Short-Term and Long-Term Goals:

Short-Term Goals:

Complete an online course on digital marketing within the next three months.

Save $1,000 for an emergency fund within the next six months.

Improve physical fitness by working out at least three times a week for the next six months.

Read one book per month for the next year to enhance personal development.

Long-Term Goals:

Achieve a managerial position in my current company within the next five years.

Buy a house within the next seven years.

Travel to at least five different countries within the next ten years.

Write and publish a book within the next ten years.

2. Develop a Step-by-Step Action Plan for One of Your Major Goals:

Choose one of your major goals and develop a detailed action plan to achieve it. Breaking down your goal into smaller, manageable steps will make it more attainable and provide a clear roadmap for success.

Steps to Develop Your Action Plan:

Define Your Goal: Clearly state your goal and ensure that it is specific, measurable, achievable, relevant, and time-bound.

Identify the Steps: Break down your goal into smaller tasks and steps that you need to complete. Be as detailed as possible.

Set Deadlines: Assign a deadline for each step to create a sense of urgency and keep yourself on track.

Monitor Your Progress: Regularly review your action plan and track your progress. Make adjustments as needed to stay on course.

Example of a Step-by-Step Action Plan:

Goal: Complete an online course on digital marketing within the next three months.

Action Plan:

Research and Choose a Course: Spend one week researching and selecting an online course that fits my needs and schedule. Deadline: [Date]

Enrol in the Course: Enrol in the chosen course and create a study schedule. Deadline: [Date]

Create a Study Plan: Break down the course modules and assignments into a weekly study plan. Allocate specific times each week to study and complete assignments. Deadline: [Date]

Stick to the Study Plan: Follow the study plan diligently, dedicating the required time each week to complete the coursework. Deadline: Ongoing until completion

Complete Assignments: Submit all assignments and projects by their respective deadlines. Deadline: Ongoing until completion

Review and Revise: Review course material regularly and revise key concepts. Deadline: Ongoing until completion

Take the Final Exam: Prepare for and take the final exam to complete the course. Deadline: [Date]

Earn the Certification: Successfully complete the course and earn the certification. Deadline: [Date]

Inspirational Quotes

Inspirational quotes can serve as powerful reminders of the importance of setting clear, specific goals and staying committed to achieving them. Here are a few quotes to inspire you:

"A goal properly set is halfway reached." – Zig Ziglar

"Goals are dreams with deadlines." – Diana Scharf Hunt

"Setting goals is the first step in turning the invisible into the visible." – Tony Robbins

"The only limit to our realization of tomorrow will be our doubts of today." – Franklin D. Roosevelt

"You are never too old to set another goal or to dream a new dream." – C.S. Lewis

Understanding SMART Goals

SMART goals are a proven framework for setting clear, specific, and achievable goals. By ensuring that your goals meet the SMART criteria, you can create a structured plan that increases your chances of success.

Specific:

A specific goal clearly defines what you want to achieve. It answers the questions: Who, What, Where, When, and Why. Being specific helps to focus your efforts and avoid ambiguity.

Example of a Specific Goal:

Vague: "Get in shape."

Specific: "Lose 10 pounds by exercising three times a week and following a healthy diet for the next three months."

Measurable:

A measurable goal includes criteria for tracking your progress and determining when you have achieved the goal. It answers the question: How will I know when I have achieved my goal?

Example of a Measurable Goal:

Vague: "Improve my finances."

Measurable: "Save $5,000 for an emergency fund within the next 12 months."

Achievable:

An achievable goal is realistic and attainable, considering your resources and constraints. It answers the question: Is this goal realistic, given my current situation?

Example of an Achievable Goal:

Vague: "Become a millionaire overnight."

Achievable: "Increase my income by 20% over the next year by taking on additional freelance work and improving my skills."

Relevant:

A relevant goal aligns with your values, long-term objectives, and priorities. It answers the question: Does this goal matter to me, and is it aligned with my overall vision?

Example of a Relevant Goal:

Vague: "Learn a new skill."

Relevant: "Learn digital marketing skills to enhance my career prospects in the marketing industry."

Time-bound:

A time-bound goal has a specific deadline, creating a sense of urgency and helping you stay focused. It answers the question: When do I want to achieve this goal?

Example of a Time-bound Goal:

Vague: "Start my own business."

Time-bound: "Launch my online store within the next six months."

Benefits of Setting Clear, Specific Goals

Setting clear, specific goals offers numerous benefits, including:

1. Provides Direction:

Clear goals provide a roadmap for your life, guiding your decisions and actions. They help you stay focused on what truly matters and avoid distractions.

2. Increases Motivation:

Having specific goals gives you a sense of purpose and motivation. It provides a reason to push through challenges and stay committed to your aspirations.

3. Enhances Focus:

Specific goals help you concentrate your efforts on what is important. They prevent you from spreading yourself too thin and ensure that your energy is directed towards meaningful activities.

4. Facilitates Planning:

Clear goals make it easier to create a structured plan for achieving them. By breaking down your goals into manageable steps, you can develop a realistic action plan.

5. Boosts Confidence:

Achieving specific goals boosts your confidence and self-esteem. Each accomplishment reinforces your belief in your abilities and motivates you to set and achieve even more ambitious goals.

6. Encourages Accountability:

Written goals hold you accountable for your actions. They serve as a constant reminder of your commitments and help you stay on track.

7. Enables Progress Tracking:

Measurable goals allow you to track your progress and celebrate your achievements. Regularly reviewing your progress helps you stay motivated and make necessary adjustments.

Overcoming Common Challenges in Goal Setting

Setting and achieving goals can be challenging, but understanding and addressing common obstacles can help you stay on track. Here are some common challenges and strategies to overcome them:

1. Lack of Clarity:

When goals are vague or unclear, it can be difficult to know where to start or what steps to take. Ensure that your goals are specific and well-defined.

Strategy: Use the SMART criteria to create clear, specific goals that provide direction and focus.

2. Procrastination:

Procrastination can prevent you from taking action and making progress towards your goals. It often stems from fear of failure, perfectionism, or feeling overwhelmed.

Strategy: Break down your goals into smaller, manageable steps and set deadlines for each task. Use tools such as to-do lists, calendars, and reminders to stay organized and accountable.

3. Lack of Motivation:

Staying motivated can be challenging, especially when progress is slow or obstacles arise. Finding ways to maintain your motivation is crucial for achieving your goals.

Strategy: Regularly review your goals and remind yourself of the reasons why you set them. Celebrate small victories and milestones along the way. Surround yourself with supportive and encouraging people who can help you stay motivated.

4. Unrealistic Goals:

Setting goals that are too ambitious or unrealistic can lead to frustration and discouragement. It's important to set goals that are challenging but attainable.

Strategy: Consider your current resources, constraints, and capabilities when setting your goals. Ensure that your goals are realistic and achievable within the given timeframe.

5. Fear of Failure:

Fear of failure can prevent you from taking risks and pursuing your goals. It's important to recognize that failure is a natural part of the learning process and can provide valuable lessons.

Strategy: Reframe failure as an opportunity for growth and learning. Embrace a growth mindset and focus on the progress you make, rather than the setbacks.

6. Lack of Support:

Having a support system can make a significant difference in your ability to achieve your goals. Without support, it can be challenging to stay motivated and overcome obstacles.

Strategy: Seek out mentors, coaches, friends, or family members who can provide guidance, encouragement, and accountability. Join groups or communities with similar goals where you can share experiences and learn from others.

Steps to Successful Goal Setting

Achieving your goals involves a series of steps that help you move from intention to action. Here's a comprehensive approach to successful goal setting:

1. Identify Your Goals

Start by identifying what you want to achieve. Consider various areas of your life, such as career, health, relationships, personal growth, finances, and leisure. Reflect on your values, passions, and long-term vision to ensure that your goals are meaningful and aligned with your overall aspirations.

2. Use the SMART Criteria

Apply the SMART criteria to each goal to ensure that it is Specific, Measurable, Achievable, Relevant, and Time-bound. This framework helps you create clear and actionable goals that provide direction and focus.

3. Write Down Your Goals

Writing down your goals solidifies your commitment and serves as a tangible reminder of your intentions. Use a journal, planner, or digital tool to record your goals and keep them visible.

4. Develop an Action Plan

Break down each goal into smaller, manageable steps. Create a detailed action plan that outlines the specific tasks you need to complete, deadlines for each task, and resources required. A well-structured action plan helps you stay organized and focused.

5. Set Deadlines

Establish deadlines for each step in your action plan to create a sense of urgency and accountability. Deadlines help you stay on track and ensure that you make consistent progress towards your goals.

6. Monitor Your Progress

Regularly review your goals and action plan to track your progress. Monitoring your progress allows you to celebrate achievements, identify areas for improvement, and make necessary adjustments.

7. Stay Flexible

Be prepared to adjust your goals and action plan as needed. Life is dynamic, and circumstances may change, requiring you to modify your approach. Stay flexible and open to new opportunities.

8. Seek Support

Surround yourself with supportive people who can provide guidance, encouragement, and accountability. Share your goals with trusted friends, family members, mentors, or coaches who can help you stay motivated and overcome challenges.

9. Celebrate Successes

Celebrate your achievements and milestones along the way. Recognizing and celebrating your progress boosts your confidence and motivation, reinforcing your commitment to your goals.

10. Reflect and Learn

Regularly reflect on your experiences and learn from both successes and setbacks. Use these insights to refine your goals, improve your strategies, and continue growing and developing.

Goal Setting Tools and Techniques

Using tools and techniques can enhance your goal-setting process and help you stay organized and focused. Here are some effective tools and techniques to consider:

1. Vision Board

A vision board is a visual representation of your goals and dreams. Creating a vision board helps you visualize your aspirations and stay motivated. Use images, words, and quotes that resonate with your goals and place the vision board in a prominent location where you can see it regularly.

2. Goal Journal

A goal journal is a dedicated space to write down your goals, action plans, and reflections. Journaling helps you clarify your thoughts, track your progress, and stay accountable. Use prompts to guide your reflections and regularly review your entries.

3. To-Do Lists

To-do lists are a simple and effective way to organize your tasks and stay on track. Break down your goals into daily, weekly, and monthly tasks, and create to-do lists to manage your workload. Prioritize tasks based on their importance and deadlines.

4. Calendars and Planners

Using calendars and planners helps you schedule your tasks and deadlines. Digital or physical planners can help you visualize your timeline, set reminders, and allocate time for each task. Regularly update your planner to stay organized and focused.

5. Accountability Partner

An accountability partner is someone who shares similar goals and can provide support, encouragement, and accountability. Regularly check in with your accountability partner to share your progress, discuss challenges, and celebrate successes.

6. SMART Goals Worksheet

A SMART goals worksheet is a structured template that helps you apply the SMART criteria to your goals. Use the worksheet to define your goals, outline specific steps, and set deadlines. Regularly review and update the worksheet to track your progress.

7. Mind Mapping

Mind mapping is a visual technique that helps you brainstorm and organize your goals and action plans. Create a mind map to explore different aspects of your goals, identify key tasks, and establish connections between different elements. Use colors, images, and keywords to enhance your mind map.

Staying Motivated and Overcoming Obstacles

Achieving your goals requires sustained motivation and the ability to overcome obstacles. Here are some strategies to help you stay motivated and navigate challenges:

1. Visualize Success

Regularly visualize yourself achieving your goals. Imagine the feelings of accomplishment, pride, and satisfaction that come with reaching your objectives. Visualization reinforces your commitment and motivates you to take action.

2. Break Goals into Smaller Steps

Large goals can be overwhelming and lead to procrastination. Break your goals into smaller, manageable steps and focus on completing one step at a time. This approach makes the process more achievable and less daunting.

3. Reward Yourself

Set up a system of rewards for achieving milestones and completing tasks. Rewards can be small treats, experiences, or activities that you enjoy. Rewarding yourself reinforces positive behavior and keeps you motivated.

4. Stay Positive

Maintain a positive mindset and focus on your progress rather than setbacks. Practice gratitude and celebrate your achievements, no matter how small. Surround yourself with positive influences and seek inspiration from books, podcasts, or motivational speakers.

5. Learn from Setbacks

Setbacks are a natural part of the goal-setting process. Instead of getting discouraged, view setbacks as learning opportunities. Reflect on what went wrong, identify areas for improvement, and adjust your approach accordingly.

6. Seek Support

Don't hesitate to seek support when needed. Reach out to friends, family members, mentors, or coaches for guidance and encouragement. Join groups or communities with similar goals where you can share experiences and learn from others.

7. Maintain Balance

While working towards your goals is important, maintaining balance in your life is crucial. Take time for self-care, relaxation, and activities that bring you joy. A balanced approach ensures that you have the energy and resilience to pursue your goals.

8. Keep a Growth Mindset

Adopt a growth mindset, which is the belief that abilities and intelligence can be developed through effort and learning. Embrace challenges, seek feedback, and view failures as opportunities for growth. A growth mindset fosters resilience and persistence.

Case Studies of Goal Setting

To further illustrate the importance and effectiveness of setting clear, specific goals, let's explore two detailed case studies:

Case Study 1: Michael Phelps

Michael Phelps, the most decorated Olympian of all time, is a prime example of the power of goal setting. From a young age, Phelps set specific goals for his swimming career, including breaking world records and winning Olympic gold medals. His coach, Bob Bowman, played a crucial role in helping Phelps set and achieve these goals.

Phelps and Bowman created a detailed training plan that included rigorous workouts, nutrition, mental conditioning, and regular goal-setting sessions. They set both short-term and long-term goals, tracking progress and making adjustments as needed.

Phelps' dedication to his goals and his commitment to a structured plan led to unprecedented success. He won 23 Olympic gold medals and set multiple world records. Phelps' story highlights the importance of setting clear, specific goals and following a disciplined approach to achieve them.

Case Study 2: Sheryl Sandberg

Sheryl Sandberg, the COO of Facebook and author of "Lean In," has demonstrated the impact of goal setting in her career and personal life. Sandberg set specific goals for her professional development, including advancing to leadership positions and advocating for gender equality in the workplace.

Throughout her career, Sandberg followed a structured approach to goal setting. She identified her long-term aspirations, set specific short-term objectives, and developed action plans to achieve them. Sandberg also sought mentorship and support from colleagues and industry leaders.

Her commitment to clear, specific goals enabled her to achieve significant milestones, including becoming the first female COO of Facebook and authoring a bestselling book. Sandberg's journey underscores the importance of setting goals that align with your values and passions and the impact of having a supportive network.

Conclusion

Setting clear, specific goals is a foundational principle for achieving success in any area of your life. By using the SMART criteria, writing down your goals, breaking them into manageable steps, and regularly reviewing your progress, you can create a structured plan that increases your chances of success.

The stories of individuals like Jim Carrey, Serena Williams, and Elon Musk demonstrate the transformative power of setting and pursuing specific goals. Their achievements highlight the importance of commitment, persistence, and adaptability in the goal-setting process.

Remember, goal setting is an ongoing process that requires dedication and reflection. Stay focused on your objectives, seek support when needed, and celebrate your progress along the way. By setting clear, specific goals and taking consistent action, you can achieve your aspirations and create a fulfilling and successful life.

Inspirational Quotes to Keep You Motivated:

"A goal properly set is halfway reached." – Zig Ziglar

"Goals are dreams with deadlines." – Diana Scharf Hunt

"Setting goals is the first step in turning the invisible into the visible." – Tony Robbins

"The only limit to our realization of tomorrow will be our doubts of today." – Franklin D. Roosevelt

"You are never too old to set another goal or to dream a new dream." – C.S. Lewis

By embracing the principles of clear, specific goal setting, you

Chapter 4: Believe in Yourself and Your Abilities

Overview

Self-belief is the cornerstone of personal and professional success. It is the confidence and assurance in your abilities, qualities, and judgment. Believing in yourself is crucial for overcoming obstacles and achieving your goals. It empowers you to take risks, pursue opportunities, and bounce back from setbacks. Confidence opens doors, enabling you to explore new possibilities and reach your full potential.

Without self-belief, even the most talented individuals can falter in the face of challenges. Conversely, those who believe in their abilities can achieve remarkable success, regardless of the obstacles they encounter. This chapter will explore the importance of self-belief, provide real-life examples of individuals who achieved success through unwavering confidence, offer practical tips for boosting your confidence, and guide you through exercises to reinforce your self-belief.

Real-Life Examples

Michael Jordan:

Michael Jordan, widely regarded as one of the greatest basketball players of all time, is a powerful example of self-belief. Despite being cut from his high school basketball team, Jordan did not let this setback deter him. Instead, he used it as motivation to work harder and prove his abilities.

Jordan's relentless determination and belief in his talent led him to become a six-time NBA champion, five-time NBA Most Valuable Player (MVP), and a two-time Olympic gold medalist. His journey from being rejected in high school to becoming a basketball legend underscores the importance of believing in oneself and persevering through challenges.

Sara Blakely:

Sara Blakely, the founder of Spanx, is another inspiring example of self-belief. Before creating Spanx, Blakely faced numerous rejections and setbacks in her career. She initially worked as a salesperson, selling fax machines door-to-door. Despite her lack of experience in the fashion industry, Blakely believed in her idea for a new type of women's undergarment that would be both comfortable and flattering.

With her savings of $5,000, Blakely developed a prototype and pitched her idea to various manufacturers and retailers. Despite many rejections, she remained confident in her vision. Her persistence paid off when she secured a deal with Neiman Marcus, and Spanx quickly became a sensation. Today, Spanx is a billion-dollar company, and Blakely is recognized as one of the most successful self-made women in the world. Her story demonstrates the power of self-belief and determination in achieving extraordinary success.

Tips for Boosting Self-Belief

1. Use Affirmations to Boost Your Confidence:

Affirmations are positive statements that reinforce your self-belief and confidence. By repeating affirmations daily, you can reprogram your subconscious mind to adopt a more positive and confident mindset. Affirmations help you focus on your strengths and abilities, boosting your self-esteem and motivation.

Examples of Affirmations:

"I am capable and confident in my abilities."

"I believe in myself and my potential to succeed."

"I embrace challenges and grow from them."

"I am worthy of success and happiness."

"I trust in my judgment and decisions."

2. Celebrate Your Achievements, No Matter How Small:

Celebrating your achievements, both big and small, reinforces your self-belief and motivates you to keep moving forward. Acknowledging your successes helps you recognize your capabilities and builds your confidence over time.

Ways to Celebrate Your Achievements:

Keep a success journal where you write down your accomplishments.

Reward yourself with a treat or a special activity when you achieve a goal.

Share your achievements with friends and family who support and encourage you.

Reflect on your progress and how far you have come.

3. Surround Yourself with Positive Influences:

The people you surround yourself with can have a significant impact on your self-belief. Positive, supportive individuals can uplift and encourage you, while negative influences can undermine your confidence. Choose to spend time with people who believe in you and inspire you to reach your full potential.

4. Challenge Negative Thoughts:

Negative self-talk can erode your confidence and self-belief. It's important to recognize and challenge these thoughts, replacing them with positive and empowering ones. Whenever you catch yourself thinking negatively, pause and reframe your thoughts in a more positive light.

Examples of Reframing Negative Thoughts:

Negative: "I can't do this."

Positive: "I can do this if I put in the effort and stay focused."

Negative: "I'm not good enough."

Positive: "I am capable and have valuable skills to offer."

5. Set Realistic and Achievable Goals:

Setting and achieving realistic goals can boost your confidence and reinforce your self-belief. Start with small, manageable goals that are within your reach, and gradually work towards larger objectives. Each success builds your confidence and demonstrates your ability to achieve your goals.

Exercises to Reinforce Self-Belief

1. Strengths Inventory:

A strengths inventory is an exercise that helps you identify and acknowledge your strengths, skills, and past successes. By focusing on your strengths, you can build your confidence and remind yourself of your capabilities.

Steps to Create a Strengths Inventory:

List Your Strengths: Write down your strengths, talents, and skills. Consider areas where you excel and activities you enjoy.

Identify Past Successes: Reflect on your past achievements and successes. Write down specific examples of times when you have succeeded or overcome challenges.

Seek Feedback: Ask friends, family, or colleagues to provide feedback on your strengths and accomplishments. Others can often see strengths that you may not recognize in yourself.

Review and Reflect: Regularly review your strengths inventory to remind yourself of your capabilities and build your confidence.

Example of a Strengths Inventory:

Strengths:

Strong communication skills

Creativity and innovation

Ability to work well under pressure

Problem-solving skills

Leadership and teamwork

Past Successes:

Successfully led a project team to complete a major client project ahead of schedule.

Developed a new marketing campaign that increased sales by 20%.

Completed a challenging certification program while working full-time.

Overcame a fear of public speaking and delivered a successful presentation at a conference.

2. Positive Affirmations:

Positive affirmations are a powerful tool for reinforcing self-belief and building confidence. By writing and repeating affirmations daily, you can cultivate a positive mindset and boost your self-esteem.

Steps to Create and Use Positive Affirmations:

Write Affirmations: Write down positive affirmations that resonate with you and reinforce your self-belief. Use present tense and positive language.

Repeat Daily: Set aside time each day to repeat your affirmations, either out loud or silently. Incorporate them into your daily routine, such as during your morning routine or before bed.

Believe in Your Affirmations: As you repeat your affirmations, believe in the words you are saying. Visualize yourself embodying the qualities and strengths described in your affirmations.

Examples of Positive Affirmations:

"I am confident and capable in everything I do."

"I believe in my ability to achieve my goals."

"I am worthy of success and happiness."

"I trust myself and my decisions."

"I embrace challenges and grow stronger from them."

The Importance of Self-Belief

Self-belief is essential for several reasons:

1. Empowers You to Take Risks:

Believing in yourself gives you the confidence to take risks and step outside of your comfort zone. When you trust in your abilities, you are more likely to seize opportunities and pursue ambitious goals.

2. Enhances Resilience:

Self-belief enhances your resilience and ability to bounce back from setbacks. When you believe in yourself, you view challenges as opportunities for growth and learning rather than insurmountable obstacles.

3. Improves Performance:

Confidence in your abilities can improve your performance in various areas of your life, including work, sports, and personal relationships. Self-belief enables you to perform at your best and achieve your full potential.

4. Attracts Positive Opportunities:

People who believe in themselves often attract positive opportunities and relationships. Confidence is an attractive quality that draws others to you, opening doors to new possibilities and collaborations.

Developing Self-Belief

Developing self-belief is a continuous process that involves cultivating a positive mindset, building confidence, and reinforcing your strengths. Here are some strategies to help you develop self-belief:

1. Set and Achieve Goals:

Setting and achieving goals, both big and small, can boost your confidence and reinforce your self-belief. Start with manageable goals that are within your reach and gradually work towards more challenging objectives.

2. Embrace a Growth Mindset:

A growth mindset is the belief that abilities and intelligence can be developed through effort and learning. Embrace challenges, seek feedback, and view failures as opportunities for growth. A growth mindset fosters resilience and self-belief.

3. Practice Self-Compassion:

Be kind and compassionate towards yourself, especially when facing setbacks or failures. Treat yourself with the same kindness and understanding that you would offer to a friend. Self-compassion helps you maintain a positive mindset and reinforces your self-belief.

4. Learn from Role Models:

Identify role models who exemplify self-belief and confidence. Study their journeys, learn from their experiences, and draw inspiration from their successes. Role models can provide valuable insights and motivation for developing your self-belief.

5. Visualize Success:

Visualization is a powerful technique for building self-belief and confidence. Regularly visualize yourself achieving your goals and experiencing success. Imagine the feelings of pride, satisfaction, and accomplishment that come with reaching your objectives.

6. Practice Positive Self-Talk:

Replace negative self-talk with positive and empowering statements. Be mindful of the language you use

Chapter 5: Adopt a Positive Mindset

Overview

A positive mindset is a mental and emotional attitude that focuses on the bright side of life and expects positive outcomes. It is more than just being cheerful or optimistic; it involves a conscious choice to cultivate an outlook that enhances well-being, resilience, and success. Adopting a positive mindset can transform your life, helping you navigate challenges more effectively, build stronger relationships, and achieve your goals.

Research shows that individuals with a positive mindset are healthier, happier, and more successful. They are better equipped to cope with stress, recover from setbacks, and maintain a sense of purpose and direction. This chapter explores the benefits of a positive mindset, provides real-life examples of individuals who turned their lives around through positivity, offers practical tips for cultivating optimism, and guides you through exercises to develop a positive outlook.

Real-Life Examples

1. Oprah Winfrey:

Oprah Winfrey's life is a testament to the power of a positive mindset. Born into poverty and facing numerous hardships, including abuse and discrimination, Oprah could have easily succumbed to negativity. Instead, she chose to focus on her dreams and aspirations.

Oprah's positive mindset fuelled her determination to succeed. She worked tirelessly, overcoming numerous obstacles to become one of the most influential media moguls in the world. Her positive outlook not only transformed her own life but also inspired millions of people worldwide. Oprah's story demonstrates that a positive mindset can lead to extraordinary success and impact.

2. J.K. Rowling:

Before J.K. Rowling became the world-renowned author of the Harry Potter series, she faced significant challenges. As a single mother living on welfare, Rowling struggled with depression and financial difficulties. Despite these hardships, she maintained a positive mindset and continued to pursue her passion for writing.

Rowling's optimism and perseverance paid off when the first Harry Potter book was published and became a global phenomenon. Her story highlights how a positive mindset, combined with determination and hard work, can turn even the most challenging circumstances into opportunities for success.

3. Nelson Mandela:

Nelson Mandela's life exemplifies the transformative power of a positive mindset. Imprisoned for 27 years for his efforts to end apartheid in South Africa, Mandela could have easily become bitter and resentful. Instead, he chose to focus on hope, reconciliation, and the vision of a free and democratic South Africa.

Mandela's positive outlook and unwavering commitment to his ideals helped him endure the hardships of imprisonment and eventually lead his country to freedom. His legacy serves as a powerful reminder that a positive mindset can overcome even the most formidable challenges and inspire lasting change.

Benefits of a Positive Mindset

Adopting a positive mindset offers numerous benefits that can enhance various aspects of your life:

1. Improved Mental Health:

A positive mindset is linked to better mental health. It reduces the risk of depression, anxiety, and stress. Positive thinking promotes emotional well-being, helping you maintain a balanced and healthy state of mind.

2. Enhanced Physical Health:

Research shows that individuals with a positive outlook are generally healthier. They have lower levels of inflammation, better cardiovascular health, and a stronger immune system. Positive thinking also contributes to healthier lifestyle choices, such as regular exercise and a balanced diet.

3. Increased Resilience:

A positive mindset enhances resilience, the ability to bounce back from setbacks and adversity. Optimistic individuals view challenges as opportunities for growth and learning, rather than insurmountable obstacles.

4. Better Relationships:

Positivity fosters better relationships. People with a positive mindset are more empathetic, supportive, and understanding. They build stronger, more meaningful connections with others and create a positive social environment.

5. Greater Success:

A positive mindset is a key driver of success. It enhances motivation, creativity, and problem-solving skills. Positive thinkers are more likely to set and achieve their goals, persevere through difficulties, and seize opportunities.

6. Increased Happiness:

Ultimately, a positive mindset leads to greater happiness and life satisfaction. Focusing on the positive aspects of life cultivates a sense of gratitude, joy, and fulfilment.

Tips for Cultivating a Positive Mindset

1. Practice Gratitude Daily:

Gratitude is a powerful tool for cultivating a positive mindset. By focusing on the things, you are grateful for, you shift your attention away from negativity and appreciate the positive aspects of your life.

Ways to Practice Gratitude:

Gratitude Journal: Keep a journal where you write down three things you are grateful for each day. Reflect on these entries regularly to reinforce positive thinking.

Gratitude Meditation: Spend a few minutes each day in meditation, focusing on the things you are grateful for. Visualize these positive aspects and feel the gratitude in your heart.

Express Gratitude: Share your gratitude with others. Thank the people in your life who have made a positive impact, and express appreciation for their support and kindness.

2. Avoid Negative Self-Talk:

Negative self-talk can undermine your confidence and perpetuate a negative mindset. Be mindful of the language you use when talking to yourself, and challenge any negative thoughts.

Strategies to Avoid Negative Self-Talk:

Reframe Negative Thoughts: When you catch yourself thinking negatively, reframe the thought in a positive light. For example, replace "I can't do this" with "I can do this if I put in the effort and stay focused."

Use Positive Affirmations: Create and repeat positive affirmations that reinforce your self-belief and confidence. Affirmations can help reprogram your subconscious mind to adopt a more positive outlook.

Be Kind to Yourself: Treat yourself with the same kindness and compassion that you would offer to a friend. Acknowledge your efforts and progress, and avoid harsh self-criticism.

3. Surround Yourself with Positive Influences:

The people you surround yourself with can significantly impact your mindset. Spend time with individuals who uplift, inspire, and support you. Positive influences can reinforce your optimism and help you maintain a positive outlook.

Ways to Surround Yourself with Positivity:

Choose Positive Relationships: Seek out relationships with people who are positive, supportive, and encouraging. Minimize contact with individuals who are consistently negative or toxic.

Join Positive Communities: Engage in communities or groups that share your interests and values. Positive communities can provide a sense of belonging and support.

Consume Positive Content: Read books, listen to podcasts, and watch videos that inspire and motivate you. Positive content can reinforce your optimism and provide valuable insights.

4. Focus on Solutions, Not Problems:

When faced with challenges, focus on finding solutions rather than dwelling on the problems. A solution-oriented mindset helps you stay proactive and positive, enabling you to overcome obstacles more effectively.

Strategies to Focus on Solutions:

Identify the Problem: Clearly define the problem you are facing. Understanding the issue is the first step toward finding a solution.

Brainstorm Solutions: Generate a list of possible solutions to the problem. Consider different approaches and evaluate their feasibility.

Take Action: Choose the best solution and take action. Break the solution into manageable steps and follow through with your plan.

Reflect and Adjust: After implementing the solution, reflect on the outcome. If the problem persists, adjust your approach and try alternative solutions.

5. Practice Mindfulness and Meditation:

Mindfulness and meditation are effective practices for cultivating a positive mindset. They help you stay present, reduce stress, and enhance your overall well-being.

Ways to Practice Mindfulness and Meditation:

Mindfulness Meditation: Set aside time each day to practice mindfulness meditation. Focus on your breath and observe your thoughts and feelings without judgment.

Body Scan Meditation: Perform a body scan meditation to bring awareness to different parts of your body. This practice helps you relax and release tension.

Gratitude Meditation: Incorporate gratitude into your meditation practice. Focus on the things you are grateful for and visualize them in your mind's eye.

Exercises to Develop a Positive Mindset

1. Keep a Gratitude Journal:

A gratitude journal is a powerful tool for cultivating a positive mindset. By regularly writing down the things you are grateful for, you train your mind to focus on the positive aspects of your life.

Steps to Keep a Gratitude Journal:

Choose a Journal: Select a notebook or digital app to use as your gratitude journal.

Set Aside Time: Dedicate a specific time each day to write in your journal. Many people find it helpful to write in the morning or before bed.

Write Down Three Things: Each day, write down three things you are grateful for. These can be big or small, such as a kind gesture from a friend, a beautiful sunset, or a personal achievement.

Reflect and Review: Regularly review your gratitude journal entries. Reflect on the positive aspects of your life and the progress you have made.

Example of a Gratitude Journal Entry:

Date: [Date]

1. I am grateful for the support and encouragement of my family.

2. I am grateful for the opportunity to learn and grow in my career.

3. I am grateful for the beautiful weather today, which allowed me to enjoy a walk in the park.

2. Identify and Challenge Negative Beliefs:

Negative beliefs can hold you back and perpetuate a negative mindset. Identifying and challenging these beliefs is essential for cultivating a positive outlook.

Steps to Identify and Challenge Negative Beliefs:

Recognize Negative Beliefs: Pay attention to negative thoughts and beliefs that arise in your mind. Write them down to bring awareness to them.

Evaluate the Evidence: Examine the evidence for and against each negative belief. Consider whether the belief is based on facts or assumptions.

Reframe the Belief: Replace the negative belief with a more positive and realistic one

Chapter 6: Take Action and Persevere

Overview

Taking consistent action and persevering through challenges are essential components of achieving success. Many people have dreams and aspirations, but it is the persistent effort and the ability to keep going despite obstacles that ultimately lead to the realization of those dreams. Success rarely happens overnight; it is the result of sustained effort, determination, and the willingness to push through difficulties.

This chapter explores the importance of taking action and the power of perseverance. It includes inspiring real-life examples of individuals who achieved their goals through unwavering persistence, practical tips for staying motivated and overcoming setbacks, and exercises to help you break down your goals into manageable actions and reflect on your experiences. By understanding and embracing these principles, you can enhance your ability to achieve your goals and create the life you desire.

Real-Life Examples

1. Thomas Edison:

Thomas Edison, one of the most prolific inventors in history, is a prime example of the power of perseverance. Edison faced numerous failures and setbacks in his quest to invent the electric light bulb. It is famously reported that he made 1,000 unsuccessful attempts before finally succeeding.

When asked about his repeated failures, Edison responded, "I have not failed. I've just found 10,000 ways that won't work." His relentless determination and refusal to give up despite countless setbacks led to the invention of the light bulb, revolutionizing the way we live. Edison's story illustrates that persistence and the willingness to learn from failures are crucial for achieving groundbreaking success.

2. J.K. Rowling:

J.K. Rowling, the author of the Harry Potter series, faced significant challenges before her books became a global phenomenon. Before achieving success, Rowling was a single mother living on welfare, struggling to make ends meet. She faced numerous rejections from publishers who doubted the potential of her story.

Despite these obstacles, Rowling continued to write and revise her manuscript, driven by her passion and belief in her story. Her perseverance paid off when Bloomsbury Publishing decided to publish the first Harry Potter book. Today, Rowling's books have sold over 500 million copies worldwide, and she is one of the most successful authors in history. Her journey highlights the importance of persistence and the transformative power of never giving up on your dreams.

3. Walt Disney:

Walt Disney, the visionary behind the Disney empire, faced numerous failures and rejections before achieving success. Early in his career, Disney was fired from a newspaper job because his editor felt he "lacked imagination and had no good ideas." He also faced bankruptcy multiple times while trying to get his animation studio off the ground.

Disney's determination and unwavering belief in his vision kept him going. He persevered through financial struggles, business failures, and personal setbacks to create some of the most beloved characters and stories in entertainment history. Disney's legacy is a testament to the power of perseverance and the importance of pursuing your passion despite obstacles.

Tips for Taking Action and Persevering

1. Take Small Steps Daily Towards Your Goals:

Breaking down your goals into small, manageable steps makes them less daunting and more achievable. Taking consistent action, even if it is just a small step each day, keeps you moving forward and builds momentum over time.

Strategies for Taking Small Steps:

Create a To-Do List: Write down the tasks you need to complete to achieve your goal. Break these tasks into smaller, manageable actions and prioritize them.

Set Daily Goals: Each day, set specific goals for what you want to accomplish. Focus on completing these tasks, and celebrate your progress.

Use Time Management Techniques: Allocate specific times each day for working on your goals. Use techniques like the Pomodoro Technique or time blocking to stay focused and productive.

2. Don't Give Up When Faced with Setbacks:

Setbacks and failures are inevitable on the path to success. It is important to view these challenges as opportunities for growth and learning rather than reasons to give up. Perseverance is about maintaining your determination and continuing to push forward despite difficulties.

Strategies for Overcoming Setbacks:

Reframe Failures: Instead of seeing failures as the end, view them as valuable learning experiences. Reflect on what went wrong and how you can improve.

Stay Positive: Maintain a positive mindset and focus on your progress rather than your setbacks. Surround yourself with supportive people who encourage you.

Adjust Your Approach: If you encounter obstacles, be flexible and willing to adjust your approach. Explore alternative strategies and solutions to overcome challenges.

3. Set Realistic and Achievable Goals:

Setting realistic and achievable goals is crucial for maintaining motivation and perseverance. Unrealistic goals can lead to frustration and discouragement, while attainable goals provide a sense of accomplishment and progress.

Strategies for Setting Realistic Goals:

Use the SMART Criteria: Ensure your goals are Specific, Measurable, Achievable, Relevant, and Time-bound. This framework helps you create clear and attainable goals.

Break Goals into Milestones: Divide larger goals into smaller milestones. Achieving these milestones provides a sense of progress and keeps you motivated.

Regularly Review and Adjust Goals: Periodically review your goals and adjust them as needed. Life is dynamic, and your goals may need to evolve with changing circumstances.

4. Stay Committed and Persistent:

Commitment and persistence are key to achieving long-term success. It is essential to stay focused on your goals and maintain your determination, even when the journey becomes challenging.

Strategies for Staying Committed:

Visualize Success: Regularly visualize yourself achieving your goals. Imagine the feelings of pride and satisfaction that come with success.

Set Reminders: Use reminders, such as sticky notes or digital notifications, to keep your goals at the forefront of your mind.

Celebrate Progress: Celebrate your achievements and progress along the way. Recognizing your successes, no matter how small, reinforces your commitment and motivation.

Exercises to Enhance Action and Perseverance

1. Break Down a Major Goal into Daily Actions:

Breaking down a major goal into daily actions makes it more manageable and achievable. This exercise helps you create a clear action plan and maintain consistent progress.

Steps to Break Down a Major Goal:

Define Your Major Goal: Clearly state your major goal and ensure it is specific, measurable, achievable, relevant, and time-bound.

Identify Key Milestones: Break down your major goal into key milestones or intermediate objectives. These milestones should represent significant progress toward your goal.

Create a Task List: For each milestone, create a list of tasks that need to be completed. Be as detailed as possible, outlining the specific actions required.

Set Daily Actions: Divide the tasks into daily actions. Determine what you need to accomplish each day to stay on track and achieve your milestones.

Example of Breaking Down a Major Goal:

Major Goal: Write and publish a book within one year.

Milestones:

Outline the Book: Create a detailed outline of the book's content. (Deadline: 1 month)

Write the First Draft: Complete the first draft of the manuscript. (Deadline: 6 months)

Revise and Edit: Revise and edit the manuscript based on feedback. (Deadline: 9 months)

Publish the Book: Prepare the manuscript for publication and publish the book. (Deadline: 12 months)

Daily Actions:

Outline the Book:

Day 1: Brainstorm and list main topics and chapters.

Day 2-7: Develop a detailed outline for each chapter.

Write the First Draft:

Day 1-30: Write 1,000 words each day to complete the first draft.

Day 31-60: Review and revise each chapter.

Revise and Edit:

Day 1-30: Seek feedback from beta readers and make revisions.

Day 31-60: Perform a final edit and proofread the manuscript.

Publish the Book:

Day 1-30: Format the manuscript for publication.

Day 31: Publish the book and begin marketing efforts.

2. Reflect on a Time You Persisted and Succeeded:

Reflecting on past experiences of persistence and success reinforces your belief in your ability to overcome challenges. This exercise helps you draw inspiration and motivation from your previous achievements.

Steps to Reflect on a Time You Persisted:

Choose a Specific Example: Think of a specific time in your life when you faced significant challenges but persisted and eventually succeeded. This could be a personal, professional, or academic experience.

Describe the Situation: Write a detailed account of the situation. Include the obstacles you encountered, the actions you took, and the strategies you used to persevere.

Identify Key Takeaways: Reflect on the key lessons you learned from the experience. Consider how your persistence contributed to your success and what you would do differently in the future.

Apply the Lessons: Think about how you can apply the lessons learned to your current goals and challenges. Use this reflection to reinforce your determination and confidence.

Example of Reflecting on Persistence and Success:

Situation: Completing a Master's Degree While Working Full-Time

Description: During my pursuit of a Master's degree, I was also working full-time in a demanding job. Balancing work, studies, and personal life was incredibly challenging. There were times when I felt overwhelmed and considered quitting the program.

Obstacles:

Managing time effectively between work and studies.

Handling stress and maintaining motivation.

Sacrificing personal time and leisure activities.

Actions Taken:

Created a detailed schedule to allocate specific times for work, study, and personal activities.

Used time management techniques like the Pomodoro Technique to maintain focus and productivity.

Sought support from colleagues, friends, and family to stay motivated and manage stress.

Key Takeaways:

Time management and organization are crucial for balancing multiple responsibilities.

Seeking support and maintaining a positive mindset are essential for perseverance.

Setting small, achievable goals helps maintain motivation and track progress.

Application:

Apply the same time management strategies to current professional projects.

Seek support from mentors and peers when facing challenging tasks.

Set clear, incremental goals to achieve long-term objectives.

The Importance of Action and Perseverance

Taking action and persevering through challenges are critical for achieving success in any endeavor. These qualities enable you to transform your goals into reality, overcome obstacles, and continue moving forward despite setbacks. Here's why action and perseverance are so important:

1. Bridges the Gap Between Goals and Outcomes:

Taking consistent action is what transforms your goals from ideas into tangible outcomes. Without action, even the best-laid plans remain unfulfilled dreams. Perseverance ensures that you continue to take action, even when progress is slow or obstacles arise.

2. Builds Resilience and Character:

Persevering through challenges builds resilience, the ability to bounce back from adversity. It also strengthens your character, teaching you patience, determination, and the value of hard work. These qualities are essential for long-term success.

3. Enhances Learning and Growth:

Facing and overcoming obstacles provides valuable learning experiences. Each challenge offers lessons that contribute to your personal and professional growth. Perseverance ensures that you continue to learn and grow, even in the face of difficulties.

4. Increases Confidence and Self-Efficacy:

Successfully taking action and persisting through challenges boosts your confidence and belief in your abilities. This increased self-efficacy empowers you to tackle even more ambitious goals and challenges in the future.

5. Fosters Creativity and Innovation:

Persistent action often requires creative problem-solving and innovative thinking. When faced with obstacles, you must find new ways to overcome them, which fosters creativity and leads to innovative solutions.

Developing the Habit of Taking Action

Developing the habit of taking consistent action requires discipline, motivation, and effective strategies. Here are some tips to help you cultivate this habit:

1. Set Clear and Specific Goals:

Clearly define your goals and ensure they are specific, measurable, achievable, relevant, and time-bound (SMART). Having well-defined goals provides direction and motivation for taking action.

2. Create a Detailed Action Plan:

Develop a detailed action plan that outlines the steps needed to achieve your goals. Break down large tasks into smaller, manageable actions and set deadlines for each step. A clear plan makes it easier to take consistent action.

3. Prioritize Your Tasks:

Identify the most important tasks that will move you closer to your goals and prioritize them. Focus on completing high-priority tasks first to ensure you are making meaningful progress.

4. Use Time Management Techniques:

Effective time management is crucial for maintaining consistent action. Techniques such as the Pomodoro Technique, time blocking, and setting specific time limits for tasks can help you stay focused and productive.

5. Stay Accountable:

Accountability helps maintain motivation and commitment. Share your goals and progress with a trusted friend, mentor, or accountability partner who can provide support and encouragement.

6. Overcome Procrastination:

Procrastination can hinder your ability to take consistent action. Identify the reasons for your procrastination and implement strategies to overcome it, such as breaking tasks into smaller steps, setting deadlines, and removing distractions.

7. Maintain a Positive Mindset:

A positive mindset is essential for staying motivated and persevering through challenges. Focus on your progress, celebrate small victories, and maintain a positive outlook on your journey.

Exercises to Enhance Perseverance

1. Visualization Exercise:

Visualization is a powerful technique that can enhance perseverance by helping you imagine the successful outcome of your efforts. This exercise helps you stay motivated and focused on your goals.

Steps for Visualization Exercise:

Find a Quiet Space: Choose a quiet and comfortable space where you can sit without distractions.

Close Your Eyes: Close your eyes and take a few deep breaths to relax and clear your mind.

Visualize Your Goal: Imagine yourself achieving your goal in vivid detail. Picture the specific steps you are taking, the challenges you are overcoming, and the final outcome.

Feel the Emotions: Focus on the positive emotions associated with achieving your goal, such as pride, satisfaction, and joy. Allow yourself to fully experience these feelings.

Reinforce the Vision: Repeat this visualization exercise regularly to reinforce your commitment and motivation.

2. Perseverance Reflection:

Reflecting on your experiences of perseverance can reinforce your belief in your ability to overcome challenges and achieve your goals. This exercise helps you draw inspiration and strength from your past successes.

Steps for Perseverance Reflection:

Recall a Challenging Experience: Think of a specific time when you faced significant challenges but persisted and eventually succeeded.

Describe the Experience: Write a detailed account of the situation, including the obstacles you encountered, the actions you took, and the strategies you used to persevere.

Identify Key Lessons: Reflect on the key lessons you learned from the experience. Consider how your persistence contributed to your success and what you would do differently in the future.

Apply the Lessons: Think about how you can apply the lessons learned to your current goals and challenges. Use this reflection to reinforce your determination and confidence.

Example of Perseverance Reflection:

Experience: Completing a Marathon

Description: I decided to run a marathon to challenge myself and improve my fitness. Training was demanding, and there were times when I felt exhausted and doubted my ability to complete the race. Injuries and busy schedules added to the difficulty.

Obstacles:

Physical exhaustion and injuries.

Balancing training with work and personal commitments.

Maintaining motivation during long training sessions.

Actions Taken:

Followed a structured training plan with gradual increases in distance.

Listened to my body and took rest days to recover from injuries.

Sought support from running groups and training partners for encouragement.

Key Lessons:

Consistency and gradual progress are key to achieving challenging goals.

Support from others can provide motivation and accountability.

Mental resilience is just as important as physical endurance.

Application:

Apply a structured and consistent approach to current professional projects.

Seek support and collaboration from colleagues and mentors.

Focus on building mental resilience through positive self-talk and visualization.

Inspirational Quotes

Inspirational quotes can serve as powerful reminders of the importance of taking action and persevering through challenges. Here are a few quotes to inspire you:

"Perseverance is not a long race; it is many short races one after the other." – Walter Elliot

"The difference between a successful person and others is not a lack of strength, not a lack of knowledge, but rather a lack in will." – Vince Lombardi

"Success is not final, failure is not fatal: It is the courage to continue that counts." – Winston Churchill

"Many of life's failures are people who did not realize how close they were to success when they gave up." – Thomas Edison

"It does not matter how slowly you go as long as you do not stop." – Confucius

Conclusion

Taking action and persevering through challenges are essential qualities for achieving success. By breaking down your goals into manageable steps, staying committed, and maintaining a positive mindset, you can overcome obstacles and continue moving forward.

The stories of individuals like Thomas Edison, J.K. Rowling, and Walt Disney demonstrate the transformative power of persistence and determination. Their achievements highlight the importance of relentless effort, learning from failures, and the willingness to push through difficulties.

Remember, success is not a destination but a journey that requires consistent action and perseverance. Embrace the challenges, learn from your experiences, and stay focused on your goals. By taking action and persevering, you can achieve your dreams and create a fulfilling and successful life.

Chapter 7: Learn from Feedback and Failures

Overview

Failure is often viewed negatively, but it is an integral part of the learning process. Embracing failure as a stepping stone rather than a stumbling block can transform your perspective and approach to challenges. When you see failure as an opportunity for growth, you open yourself up to invaluable lessons and experiences that can propel you toward greater success. Similarly, feedback—whether positive or constructive—is a critical tool for personal and professional development. By learning to seek, accept, and act on feedback, you can continually improve and refine your skills and strategies.

This chapter delves into the importance of learning from feedback and failures, offering real-life examples of individuals who turned their failures into successes, practical tips for viewing failures positively, and exercises to help you reflect on your experiences and seek constructive feedback. By understanding and embracing these principles, you can develop resilience, adaptability, and a growth mindset that will serve you well in all aspects of life.

Real-Life Examples

1. Steve Jobs:

Steve Jobs, the co-founder of Apple Inc., faced significant failures early in his career. In 1985, Jobs was ousted from Apple, the company he had co-founded, due to a power struggle within the company. This could have been a devastating blow, but Jobs used this setback as an opportunity for growth and learning.

During his time away from Apple, Jobs founded NeXT, a computer platform development company, and purchased The Graphics Group, which later became Pixar Animation Studios. His experiences and innovations during this period were crucial in shaping his vision and approach. When he returned to Apple in 1997, Jobs revitalized the company, leading it to become one of the most successful and influential technology companies in the world. His story exemplifies how embracing failure and learning from it can lead to greater achievements.

2. J.K. Rowling:

J.K. Rowling, the author of the Harry Potter series, faced numerous rejections before achieving literary success. Before her first book was published, Rowling was a struggling single mother living on welfare. Her manuscript for "Harry Potter and the Philosopher's Stone" was rejected by twelve publishers.

Instead of giving up, Rowling persevered, eventually securing a publishing deal with Bloomsbury. The Harry Potter series went on to become a global phenomenon, selling over 500 million copies and making Rowling one of the most successful authors in history. Her journey highlights the importance of resilience and the willingness to learn from rejection and failure.

3. Thomas Edison:

Thomas Edison, one of the most prolific inventors of all time, is well-known for his perseverance in the face of failure. Edison famously failed thousands of times while trying to invent the electric light bulb. When asked about his failures, Edison reportedly said, "I have not failed. I've just found 10,000 ways that won't work."

Edison's relentless pursuit of his goal and his ability to learn from each failure eventually led to the successful invention of the light bulb, which revolutionized the world. His story underscores the value of persistence and viewing failures as part of the journey to success.

Tips for Learning from Feedback and Failures

1. View Failures as Learning Opportunities:

Shifting your perspective on failure can have a profound impact on your ability to learn and grow. Instead of seeing failure as a negative outcome, view it as a valuable learning experience.

Strategies to View Failures Positively:

Reframe the Situation: Instead of thinking, "I failed," reframe your thought to, "What can I learn from this experience?"

Focus on Growth: Consider how the failure can help you grow and improve. Identify specific lessons and areas for development.

Embrace a Growth Mindset: Adopt a mindset that views abilities and intelligence as malleable. Believe that you can improve and succeed through effort and learning.

2. Seek Constructive Feedback:

Constructive feedback is essential for continuous improvement. Actively seeking feedback from others can provide valuable insights into your performance and areas where you can enhance your skills.

Strategies to Seek and Use Feedback:

Ask Specific Questions: When seeking feedback, ask specific questions that focus on particular aspects of your performance. This can help you get more detailed and actionable feedback.

Listen Actively: Pay close attention to the feedback you receive without interrupting or becoming defensive. Understand the feedback fully before responding.

Act on Feedback: Use the feedback to make concrete improvements. Develop a plan to address the areas highlighted and track your progress.

3. Reflect on Your Experiences:

Regular reflection on your experiences, both successes and failures, can help you gain deeper insights and improve your future performance. Reflection allows you to analyze what worked, what didn't, and how you can do better next time.

Strategies for Effective Reflection:

Keep a Learning Journal: Maintain a journal where you document your experiences, insights, and lessons learned. Reflect on both successes and failures.

Schedule Regular Reflection Time: Set aside regular time for reflection, such as at the end of each day or week. Use this time to review your actions and outcomes.

Ask Reflective Questions: Use questions like, "What did I learn from this experience?" "What could I have done differently?" and "How can I apply this lesson in the future?"

4. Develop Resilience:

Resilience is the ability to bounce back from setbacks and failures. Building resilience helps you stay focused and motivated, even when faced with challenges.

Strategies to Build Resilience:

Maintain a Positive Attitude: Focus on the positive aspects of situations and maintain a hopeful outlook. Positive thinking can boost your resilience.

Practice Self-Compassion: Be kind to yourself when you experience failure. Recognize that setbacks are a natural part of the learning process.

Build a Support Network: Surround yourself with supportive people who can offer encouragement and perspective during difficult times.

Exercises to Learn from Feedback and Failures

1. Reflect on a Failure and What You Learned from It:

Reflecting on a failure can help you extract valuable lessons and insights that contribute to your growth. This exercise encourages you to analyze a past failure and identify the key takeaways.

Steps for Reflection Exercise:

Choose a Specific Failure: Think of a specific time when you experienced a significant failure. This could be a personal, professional, or academic experience.

Describe the Situation: Write a detailed account of the situation, including what happened, the actions you took, and the outcome.

Identify Key Lessons: Reflect on what you learned from the experience. Consider what you would do differently in the future and how you can apply these lessons to current and future challenges.

Develop an Action Plan: Create a plan for how you will use the insights gained from this reflection to improve your performance and approach to similar situations.

Example of Reflecting on a Failure:

Situation: Failing to Secure a Promotion

Description: I applied for a promotion at work but was not selected. Despite my hard work and preparation, another candidate was chosen for the position.

Key Lessons:

Importance of Feedback: Seek feedback from the hiring manager to understand the reasons for not being selected. Use this feedback to identify areas for improvement.

Continuous Improvement: Focus on developing the skills and qualifications needed for the next promotion opportunity. Take relevant courses and seek new responsibilities to enhance my experience.

Networking: Build stronger relationships with colleagues and mentors who can provide support and guidance in my career development.

Action Plan:

Seek Feedback: Schedule a meeting with the hiring manager to discuss my application and areas for improvement.

Develop Skills: Enroll in a leadership training course and take on a new project at work to gain additional experience.

Build Relationships: Attend networking events and seek mentorship from senior colleagues.

2. Ask for Feedback on a Recent Project or Task:

Seeking feedback on a recent project or task can provide valuable insights into your performance and areas for improvement. This exercise encourages you to actively seek constructive feedback and use it to enhance your skills.

Steps for Feedback Exercise:

Choose a Recent Project or Task: Select a specific project or task you have recently completed and for which you would like feedback.

Identify Feedback Sources: Determine who can provide meaningful feedback. This could include supervisors, colleagues, clients, or mentors.

Ask Specific Questions: Prepare specific questions to ask when seeking feedback. Focus on areas where you want to improve or gain insights.

Listen and Reflect: Listen carefully to the feedback without interrupting or becoming defensive. Reflect on the feedback and identify actionable steps to address the areas highlighted.

Example of Asking for Feedback:

Project: Leading a Team Presentation

Feedback Sources: Supervisor, team members, and clients

Questions to Ask:

What did you think went well during the presentation?

Are there any areas where I could improve my presentation skills?

How effectively did I communicate the key points?

What suggestions do you have for future presentations?

Listening and Reflecting:

Positive Feedback: Received compliments on clear communication and engaging delivery.

Constructive Feedback: Suggestions to improve slide design and incorporate more data to support key points.

Action Plan:

Improve Slide Design: Take an online course on effective presentation design and apply new techniques to future presentations.

Incorporate Data: Work with the data analysis team to include relevant data and statistics in future presentations.

The Importance of Feedback and Failure in Growth

Feedback and failure are invaluable components of the growth process. Embracing these elements can significantly enhance your personal and professional development. Here's why they are so important:

1. Provides Objective Insights:

Feedback offers an external perspective on your performance, highlighting strengths and areas for improvement that you may not recognize. This objective insight is crucial for continuous growth and development.

2. Encourages Self-Reflection:

Receiving feedback and experiencing failure prompt you to reflect on your actions and decisions. This reflection helps you understand what worked, what didn't, and how you can improve.

3. Fosters Resilience and Adaptability:

Learning from feedback and failure builds resilience and adaptability. It teaches you to bounce back from setbacks, adjust your approach, and continue moving forward despite challenges.

4. Enhances Problem-Solving Skills:

Feedback and failure often highlight specific problems or areas that need improvement. Addressing these issues enhances your problem-solving skills and ability to navigate complex situations.

5. Promotes a Growth Mindset:

Embracing feedback and failure fosters a growth mindset, the belief that abilities and intelligence can be developed through effort and learning. A growth mindset encourages you to view challenges as opportunities for growth rather than threats.

Developing a Positive Approach to Feedback and Failure

Developing a positive approach to feedback and failure involves cultivating specific attitudes and practices that enable you to learn and grow from these experiences. Here are some tips to help you develop this positive approach:

1. Embrace a Learning Attitude:

Approach feedback and failure with a mindset focused on learning and growth. Recognize that every experience, whether positive or negative, offers valuable lessons that contribute to your development.

2. Separate Self-Worth from Performance:

Understand that failure or critical feedback does not reflect your worth as a person. Separate your self-worth from your performance and view feedback and failure as opportunities to improve, not as judgments of your value.

3. Seek Diverse Perspectives:

Actively seek feedback from a diverse range of sources. Different perspectives can provide a more comprehensive understanding of your performance and areas for improvement.

4. Practice Self-Compassion:

Be kind and compassionate towards yourself when you receive feedback or experience failure. Acknowledge your efforts and recognize that setbacks are a natural part of the growth process.

5. Implement Feedback Constructively:

Use the feedback you receive to make concrete improvements. Develop a plan to address the areas highlighted and track your progress over time. Constructive implementation of feedback leads to continuous improvement and development.

Exercises to Enhance Learning from Feedback and Failures

1. Feedback Journal:

A feedback journal is a tool for documenting and reflecting on the feedback you receive. This exercise helps you keep track of feedback, analyse it, and develop action plans for improvement.

Steps for Keeping a Feedback Journal:

Choose a Journal: Select a notebook or digital app to use as your feedback journal.

Document Feedback: Record the feedback you receive, including the source, context, and specific comments.

Analyse Feedback: Reflect on the feedback and identify common themes, strengths, and areas for improvement.

Develop Action Plans: Create action plans to address the feedback. Set specific, measurable goals for improvement and track your progress.

Example of a Feedback Journal Entry:

Date: [Date]

Source: Supervisor

Context: Performance Review

Feedback:

Strengths: Strong communication skills, effective team collaboration, and excellent project management.

Areas for Improvement: Need to improve time management and prioritize tasks more effectively.

Reflection:

Communication and collaboration are key strengths to build on.

Time management is an area that requires focused attention and improvement.

Action Plan:

Enrol in a time management course and implement new techniques to prioritize tasks.

Use a daily planner to schedule and track tasks and deadlines.

2. Failure Analysis:

Failure analysis involves a systematic review of a failure to identify the root causes and lessons learned. This exercise helps you gain deeper insights into your failures and develop strategies to avoid similar mistakes in the future.

Steps for Failure Analysis:

Select a Failure: Choose a specific failure that you want to analyse. This could be a personal, professional, or academic experience.

Describe the Failure: Write a detailed account of the failure, including what happened, the actions you took, and the outcome.

Identify Root Causes: Analyse the factors that contributed to the failure. Consider both internal factors (e.g., skills, decisions) and external factors (e.g., circumstances, resources).

Extract Lessons Learned: Identify the key lessons you learned from the failure. Reflect on how these lessons can inform your future actions and decisions.

Develop Preventive Strategies: Create strategies to prevent similar failures in the future. Develop a plan for how you will apply the lessons learned to improve your performance.

Example of Failure Analysis:

Failure: Launching a Product That Did Not Meet Sales Expectations

Description: I led the launch of a new product that did not meet sales expectations. Despite initial excitement, the product failed to gain traction in the market.

Root Causes:

Insufficient market research: The product did not fully address customer needs and preferences.

Ineffective marketing strategy: The marketing campaign did not effectively reach the target audience.

Lack of post-launch support: Limited customer support and follow-up after the launch.

Lessons Learned:

Importance of thorough market research: Ensure that products align with customer needs and preferences.

Effective marketing strategies: Develop targeted marketing campaigns that effectively reach and engage the audience.

Post-launch support: Provide robust customer support and follow-up to address any issues and build customer loyalty.

Preventive Strategies:

Conduct comprehensive market research before launching new products.

Develop and test marketing strategies to ensure they effectively reach the target audience.

Implement a post-launch support plan to provide ongoing customer support and engagement.

Inspirational Quotes

Inspirational quotes can serve as powerful reminders of the importance of learning from feedback and failures. Here are a few quotes to inspire you:

"Failure is simply the opportunity to begin again, this time more intelligently." – Henry Ford

"The only real mistake is the one from which we learn nothing." – Henry Ford

"Success is not final, failure is not fatal: It is the courage to continue that counts." – Winston Churchill

"I've failed over and over and over again in my life. And that is why I succeed." – Michael Jordan

"It's not how far you fall, but how high you bounce that counts." – Zig Ziglar

Conclusion

Understanding that failure is a part of the learning process and embracing feedback as a tool for growth are essential for personal and professional development. By viewing failures as opportunities for learning, seeking constructive feedback, and reflecting on your experiences, you can continuously improve and achieve greater success.

The stories of individuals like Steve Jobs, J.K. Rowling, and Thomas Edison demonstrate the transformative power of embracing failure and learning from it. Their journeys highlight the importance of resilience, perseverance, and the willingness to adapt and grow.

Remember, feedback and failure are not endpoints but stepping stones on the path to success. Embrace them with an open mind and a positive attitude, and use them to fuel your growth and development. By learning from feedback and failures, you can unlock your full potential and create a fulfilling and successful life.

Chapter 8: Surround Yourself with Positive Influences

Overview

The people you surround yourself with play a crucial role in shaping your mindset, behaviour, and success. Positive influences can inspire, motivate, and support you in achieving your goals, while negative influences can drain your energy and hinder your progress. Building a network of positive, supportive individuals is essential for personal and professional growth.

Surrounding yourself with positive influences involves cultivating relationships with people who uplift and encourage you, seeking out mentors and role models, and being mindful of the impact others have on your life. This chapter explores the importance of positive influences, provides real-life examples of individuals who attribute their success to supportive networks, offers practical tips for building and maintaining positive relationships, and guides you through exercises to enhance your network.

Real-Life Examples

1. Richard Branson:

Richard Branson, the founder of the Virgin Group, attributes much of his success to the positive people he surrounds himself with. Throughout his career, Branson has emphasized the importance of building strong, supportive relationships with his team, mentors, and peers. He believes that surrounding himself with positive, motivated individuals has been a key factor in his ability to innovate and grow his business empire.

Branson's approach to leadership and collaboration is characterized by his focus on creating a positive and inclusive work environment. He values input from diverse perspectives and encourages his team to think creatively and take risks. By fostering a culture of support and positivity, Branson has built a network of individuals who share his vision and drive for success.

2. Sheryl Sandberg:

Sheryl Sandberg, the Chief Operating Officer of Facebook and author of "Lean In," emphasizes the importance of mentorship and a supportive network in achieving success. Sandberg credits her mentors and the positive influences in her life for helping her navigate the challenges of her career and rise to leadership positions.

In her book "Lean In," Sandberg discusses the value of having mentors who can provide guidance, feedback, and encouragement. She also highlights the importance of building a supportive network of peers who can offer mutual support and collaboration. Sandberg's success story underscores the impact of surrounding oneself with positive influences and seeking out mentorship.

3. Oprah Winfrey:

Oprah Winfrey, one of the most influential media moguls in the world, has consistently surrounded herself with positive influences throughout her career. Winfrey credits her success to the supportive relationships she has cultivated with mentors, colleagues, and friends.

Winfrey's commitment to positivity and support is evident in her approach to business and personal growth. She often emphasizes the importance of surrounding oneself with people who uplift and inspire. By building a network of positive influences, Winfrey has been able to overcome challenges and achieve extraordinary success.

Tips for Cultivating Positive Relationships

1. Cultivate Relationships with People Who Uplift and Support You:

Building relationships with individuals who uplift and support you is essential for maintaining a positive mindset and achieving your goals. These relationships provide encouragement, motivation, and a sense of belonging.

Strategies for Cultivating Positive Relationships:

Identify Positive Influences: Take note of the people in your life who consistently uplift and support you. These individuals are likely to be positive influences.

Invest Time and Effort: Building and maintaining positive relationships requires time and effort. Make a conscious effort to spend time with and support these individuals.

Communicate Openly: Open and honest communication is key to building strong relationships. Share your goals, challenges, and successes with your positive influences and be receptive to their input.

2. Seek Out Mentors and Role Models:

Mentors and role models can provide invaluable guidance, support, and inspiration. Seeking out individuals who have achieved success in areas you aspire to can help you navigate your own journey.

Strategies for Finding Mentors and Role Models:

Identify Potential Mentors: Look for individuals in your field or industry who have achieved the success you aspire to. Consider their values, experience, and willingness to mentor.

Reach Out: Don't hesitate to reach out to potential mentors. Express your admiration for their work and explain why you are seeking their guidance.

Build Genuine Relationships: Focus on building genuine relationships with your mentors. Show appreciation for their time and insights, and be open to learning from their experiences.

3. Be Mindful of Negative Influences:

Negative influences can have a detrimental impact on your mindset and progress. It's important to be mindful of the people who drain your energy or undermine your confidence.

Strategies for Managing Negative Influences:

Set Boundaries: Establish clear boundaries with negative influences to protect your well-being. Limit your interactions with individuals who consistently bring negativity into your life.

Focus on Positivity: Surround yourself with positive influences and focus on building relationships with individuals who uplift and support you.

Practice Self-Care: Take care of your mental and emotional well-being by engaging in activities that bring you joy and fulfilment. This can help you stay resilient in the face of negativity.

4. Engage in Positive Communities:

Joining positive communities can provide a sense of belonging and support. These communities offer opportunities for networking, collaboration, and mutual encouragement.

Strategies for Engaging in Positive Communities:

Join Professional Organizations: Become a member of professional organizations related to your field or industry. These organizations often provide networking opportunities, resources, and support.

Participate in Online Communities: Engage in online communities and forums where like-minded individuals share ideas, experiences, and support.

Attend Events and Workshops: Attend events, workshops, and conferences that align with your interests and goals. These gatherings offer opportunities to connect with positive influences and expand your network.

Exercises to Enhance Your Network

1. Network Map:

Creating a network map helps you visualize your current network and identify areas for improvement. This exercise allows you to see the positive influences in your life and identify gaps where you can build new relationships.

Steps for Creating a Network Map:

Draw Your Network: Start by drawing a central circle labeled "Me" in the middle of a blank sheet of paper. Around this central circle, draw additional circles to represent the people in your network. Connect these circles with lines to show the relationships.

Label Relationships: Label each circle with the name of the person and their relationship to you (e.g., friend, mentor, colleague).

Highlight Positive Influences: Use a highlighter or different color to mark the circles that represent positive influences in your life. These are individuals who uplift, support, and inspire you.

Identify Gaps: Look for areas where you can improve your network. Identify relationships that need strengthening and areas where you can seek new positive influences.

Develop an Action Plan: Create a plan to enhance your network. This may include reaching out to potential mentors, joining new communities, or investing more time in existing positive relationships.

Example of a Network Map:

Me

Friend: Sarah (Positive Influence)

Colleague: John (Needs Strengthening)

Mentor: Lisa (Positive Influence)

Family: Mom (Positive Influence)

Professional Contact: Mark (Potential Mentor)

Action Plan:

Strengthen Relationship with John: Schedule regular coffee meetings to discuss work and share insights.

Reach Out to Mark: Send an email to Mark expressing interest in his work and requesting a meeting for mentorship.

Join a Professional Organization: Research and join a relevant professional organization to expand the network and connect with positive influences.

2. Mentor Outreach:

Identifying and reaching out to potential mentors can provide valuable guidance and support for your personal and professional growth. This exercise helps you take proactive steps to find and connect with mentors.

Steps for Mentor Outreach:

Identify Potential Mentors: Make a list of individuals who have achieved success in areas you aspire to. Consider their experience, values, and willingness to mentor.

Research Their Background: Learn more about their work, achievements, and contributions. Understanding their background helps you craft a personalized and meaningful outreach message.

Craft a Personalized Message: Write a thoughtful message expressing your admiration for their work and explaining why you are seeking their guidance. Be specific about what you hope to learn from them.

Reach Out: Send your message via email, LinkedIn, or another appropriate platform. Be respectful of their time and express gratitude for their consideration.

Follow Up: If you do not receive a response, follow up politely after a reasonable period. Persistence shows your commitment and interest in their mentorship.

Example of a Mentor Outreach Message:

Subject: Seeking Your Guidance and Mentorship

Dear [Potential Mentor's Name],

I hope this message finds you well. My name is [Your Name], and I am [Your Current Position/Role]. I have been following your work for some time, and I am truly inspired by your achievements in [specific area or field].

I am reaching out to you because I am passionate about [specific goal or interest], and I believe your insights and experience would be invaluable to my growth. I would be honored if you would consider being my mentor and providing guidance as I navigate my journey.

I understand that your time is incredibly valuable, and I am grateful for any opportunity to learn from you. If you are open to it, I would love to schedule a brief meeting at your convenience to discuss this further.

Thank you for considering my request. I look forward to the possibility of learning from you.

Best regards,

[Your Name]

The Importance of Positive Influences

Surrounding yourself with positive influences is crucial for several reasons:

1. Enhances Motivation and Confidence:

Positive influences inspire and motivate you to pursue your goals and dreams. Their encouragement boosts your confidence and helps you stay focused and determined.

2. Provides Support and Encouragement:

Having a supportive network provides a safety net during challenging times. Positive influences offer emotional support, practical advice, and encouragement when you need it most.

3. Fosters Personal and Professional Growth:

Mentors and positive role models provide valuable insights and guidance that contribute to your growth. They share their experiences, knowledge, and wisdom, helping you navigate your journey more effectively.

4. Encourages Positive Behaviours:

Being around positive influences encourages you to adopt positive behaviours and attitudes. Their example sets a standard for you to emulate, leading to personal and professional improvement.

5. Expands Opportunities:

A strong network of positive influences opens doors to new opportunities. They can introduce you to valuable contacts, recommend you for projects, and provide opportunities for collaboration and advancement.

Developing and Maintaining Positive Relationships

Developing and maintaining positive relationships requires intentional effort and a commitment to mutual support. Here are some strategies to help you cultivate and sustain positive relationships:

1. Show Genuine Interest and Appreciation:

Take an active interest in the lives and interests of the people you wish to build relationships with. Show appreciation for their contributions and achievements.

Strategies:

Listen Actively: Pay attention to what others are saying and show genuine interest in their thoughts and feelings.

Express Gratitude: Regularly express gratitude for the support and encouragement you receive. A simple thank you can go a long way.

Celebrate Successes: Celebrate the achievements and milestones of those in your network. Acknowledge their successes and show that you are genuinely happy for them.

2. Offer Support and Help:

Building strong relationships is a two-way street. Offer your support and assistance to others whenever possible.

Strategies:

Be Available: Be there for others during times of need. Offer a listening ear, practical advice, or help with tasks.

Share Resources: Share valuable information, resources, or contacts that can benefit others in your network.

Collaborate: Look for opportunities to collaborate on projects or initiatives. Working together can strengthen your bond and create mutual benefits.

3. Communicate Regularly:

Maintaining regular communication helps keep relationships strong and ensures that you stay connected with the positive influences in your life.

Strategies:

Schedule Check-Ins: Set aside regular times to check in with your network. This could be through phone calls, video chats, or in-person meetings.

Send Updates: Share updates about your progress, goals, and experiences. Keeping others informed helps maintain a sense of connection.

Be Responsive: Respond promptly to messages and requests. Being responsive shows that you value the relationship and are committed to staying connected.

4. Be Authentic and Honest:

Authenticity and honesty are key to building trust and respect in any relationship.

Strategies:

Be Yourself: Be true to who you are and let others see the real you. Authenticity fosters genuine connections.

Be Honest: Communicate openly and honestly, even when it's difficult. Honest communication builds trust and credibility.

Respect Boundaries: Respect the boundaries and preferences of others. Understanding and honoring boundaries strengthens relationships.

5. Seek Continuous Improvement:

Continuously seek ways to improve and grow in your relationships. Reflect on your interactions and look for areas where you can enhance your communication, support, and connection.

Strategies:

Solicit Feedback: Ask for feedback on how you can be a better friend, colleague, or mentor. Use this feedback to improve your interactions.

Reflect on Your Actions: Regularly reflect on your actions and behaviours. Consider how they impact your relationships and make adjustments as needed.

Invest in Personal Growth: Invest in your own personal growth and development. As you grow, you can offer more value and support to your network.

Exercises to Strengthen Positive Influences

1. Network Map Exercise:

Creating a network map helps you visualize your current network, identify positive influences, and highlight areas for improvement.

Steps:

Draw Your Network: Start with a central circle labelled "Me" on a blank sheet of paper. Around this circle, draw additional circles to represent the people in your network. Connect these circles with lines to show relationships.

Label Relationships: Label each circle with the name and relationship (e.g., friend, mentor, colleague).

Highlight Positive Influences: Use a different colour or highlighter to mark the circles representing positive influences.

Identify Gaps: Look for areas where you can strengthen your network or build new positive relationships.

Create an Action Plan: Develop a plan to enhance your network by strengthening existing relationships and seeking out new positive influences.

Example of a Network Map:

Me

Friend: Sarah (Positive Influence)

Colleague: John (Needs Strengthening)

Mentor: Lisa (Positive Influence)

Family: Mom (Positive Influence)

Professional Contact: Mark (Potential Mentor)

Action Plan:

Strengthen Relationship with John: Schedule regular coffee meetings to discuss work and share insights.

Reach Out to Mark: Send an email to Mark expressing interest in his work and requesting a meeting for mentorship.

Join a Professional Organization: Research and join a relevant professional organization to expand the network and connect with positive influences.

2. Mentor Outreach Exercise:

Identifying and reaching out to potential mentors can provide valuable guidance and support. This exercise helps you take proactive steps to connect with mentors.

Steps:

Identify Potential Mentors: Make a list of individuals who have achieved success in areas you aspire to. Consider their experience, values, and willingness to mentor.

Research Their Background: Learn more about their work, achievements, and contributions.

Craft a Personalized Message: Write a thoughtful message expressing your admiration for their work and explaining why you are seeking their guidance.

Reach Out: Send your message via email, LinkedIn, or another appropriate platform.

Follow Up: If you do not receive a response, follow up politely after a reasonable period. Persistence shows your commitment.

Example of a Mentor Outreach Message:

Subject: Seeking Your Guidance and Mentorship

Dear [Potential Mentor's Name],

I hope this message finds you well. My name is [Your Name], and I am [Your Current Position/Role]. I have been following your work for some time, and I am truly inspired by your achievements in [specific area or field].

I am reaching out to you because I am passionate about [specific goal or interest], and I believe your insights and experience would be invaluable to my growth. I would be honored if you would consider being my mentor and providing guidance as I navigate my journey.

I understand that your time is incredibly valuable, and I am grateful for any opportunity to learn from you. If you are open to it, I would love to schedule a brief meeting at your convenience to discuss this further.

Thank you for considering my request. I look forward to the possibility of learning from you.

Best regards,

[Your Name]

The Benefits of Surrounding Yourself with Positive Influences

Surrounding yourself with positive influences offers numerous benefits for your personal and professional life:

1. Increased Motivation and Confidence:

Positive influences inspire and motivate you to pursue your goals and dreams. Their encouragement boosts your confidence and helps you stay focused and determined.

2. Enhanced Personal Growth:

Positive influences provide valuable insights and guidance that contribute to your growth. They share their experiences, knowledge, and wisdom, helping you navigate your journey more effectively.

3. Better Emotional Well-Being:

Supportive relationships contribute to better emotional well-being. Positive influences offer emotional support, practical advice, and encouragement, helping you cope with stress and challenges.

4. Greater Success:

A strong network of positive influences opens doors to new opportunities. They can introduce you to valuable contacts, recommend you for projects, and provide opportunities for collaboration and advancement.

5. Improved Problem-Solving:

Positive influences offer diverse perspectives and creative solutions to challenges. Their input helps you approach problems more effectively and make better decisions.

Inspirational Quotes

Inspirational quotes can serve as powerful reminders of the importance of surrounding yourself with positive influences. Here are a few quotes to inspire you:

"Surround yourself with only people who are going to lift you higher." – Oprah Winfrey

"You are the average of the five people you spend the most time with." – Jim Rohn

"Keep away from those who try to belittle your ambitions. Small people always do that, but the really great make you believe that you too can become great." – Mark Twain

"The people you surround yourself with influence your behaviours, so choose friends who have healthy habits." – Dan Buettner

"Surround yourself with people who believe in your dreams, encourage your ideas, support your ambitions, and bring out the best in you." – Roy T. Bennett

Conclusion

The people you surround yourself with have a significant impact on your mindset, behavior, and success. Building a network of positive influences is essential for personal and professional growth. By cultivating relationships with people who uplift and support you, seeking out mentors and role models, and being mindful of the impact others have on your life, you can create a supportive and empowering environment that helps you achieve your goals.

The stories of individuals like Richard Branson, Sheryl Sandberg, and Oprah Winfrey demonstrate the transformative power of positive influences. Their successes highlight the importance of surrounding yourself with people who inspire, motivate, and support you.

Remember, building and maintaining positive relationships requires intentional effort and a commitment to mutual support. By investing in these relationships, you can enhance your motivation, confidence, and overall well-being. Surround yourself with positive influences, and you will be better equipped to navigate challenges, seize opportunities, and achieve your dreams.

Chapter 9: Practice Gratitude and Visualization

Overview

Gratitude and visualization are powerful practices that can significantly enhance your success, well-being, and overall quality of life. While gratitude involves recognizing and appreciating the positive aspects of your life, visualization focuses on imagining and mentally rehearsing your desired outcomes. Both practices can help you cultivate a positive mindset, increase your motivation, and improve your ability to achieve your goals.

This chapter explores the benefits of gratitude and visualization, provides real-life examples of individuals who have successfully used these techniques, offers practical tips for incorporating these practices into your daily routine, and guides you through exercises to help you harness the power of gratitude and visualization.

The Power of Gratitude

Gratitude is the practice of acknowledging and appreciating the good things in your life. It involves focusing on what you have rather than what you lack, and recognizing the contributions of others and the positive experiences you encounter. Gratitude has been shown to have numerous benefits for mental, emotional, and physical well-being.

Benefits of Gratitude:

Improved Mental Health: Gratitude can reduce symptoms of depression and anxiety, enhance overall mood, and increase feelings of happiness and life satisfaction.

Enhanced Relationships: Expressing gratitude can strengthen relationships by fostering positive interactions, building trust, and increasing feelings of connectedness.

Increased Resilience: Practicing gratitude can improve your ability to cope with stress and adversity, helping you to bounce back from challenges more effectively.

Better Physical Health: Gratitude has been linked to better sleep, lower blood pressure, and a stronger immune system.

Greater Life Satisfaction: Focusing on the positive aspects of your life can enhance your overall sense of well-being and fulfilment.

The Power of Visualization

Visualization involves creating vivid mental images of your desired outcomes. This practice helps you to mentally rehearse your goals, build confidence, and enhance your motivation. Visualization is widely used by athletes, performers, and successful individuals to improve performance and achieve their objectives.

Benefits of Visualization:

Enhanced Goal Achievement: Visualization helps you to clarify your goals, develop a clear plan of action, and stay focused on achieving your objectives.

Increased Confidence: Mentally rehearsing your success can boost your confidence and reduce self-doubt.

Improved Performance: Visualization can enhance your skills and performance by creating neural pathways in your brain that mimic the actual experience of achieving your goals.

Reduced Stress and Anxiety: Visualization can help to reduce stress and anxiety by providing a sense of control and calmness.

Greater Motivation: Visualizing your desired outcomes can increase your motivation and determination to take action.

Real-Life Examples

1. Jim Carrey:

Jim Carrey, the famous actor and comedian, is known for his use of visualization and gratitude to achieve his goals. Early in his career, Carrey wrote himself a check for $10 million for "acting services rendered" and dated it for Thanksgiving 1995. He kept the check in his wallet and visualized himself receiving that amount of money.

Carrey's visualization practice paid off when he received a $10 million payment for his role in the film "Dumb and Dumber" in 1994, just before Thanksgiving 1995. Carrey has often spoken about the power of visualization and gratitude in his journey to success, emphasizing the importance of believing in your dreams and being grateful for what you have.

2. Oprah Winfrey:

Oprah Winfrey, one of the most influential media moguls in the world, has long practiced gratitude and visualization. Winfrey maintains a gratitude journal, where she writes down things she is grateful for each day. This practice has helped her maintain a positive mindset and focus on the positive aspects of her life.

Winfrey also uses visualization to achieve her goals. She visualizes her desired outcomes and mentally rehearses her success. Winfrey's commitment to gratitude and visualization has played a significant role in her achievements and overall well-being.

3. Michael Phelps:

Michael Phelps, the most decorated Olympian of all time, has used visualization as a key part of his training and performance. Phelps visualized every aspect of his races, from the start to the finish, including potential challenges and how he would overcome them.

By mentally rehearsing his races, Phelps built confidence and prepared himself for various scenarios. His visualization practice contributed to his outstanding performance and numerous Olympic gold medals.

Tips for Practicing Gratitude and Visualization

1. Visualize Your Goals Daily:

Incorporate visualization into your daily routine by setting aside time each day to mentally rehearse your goals and desired outcomes.

Strategies for Effective Visualization:

Create a Clear Mental Image: Visualize your goals with as much detail as possible. Imagine the sights, sounds, feelings, and emotions associated with achieving your goals.

Use All Your Senses: Engage all your senses in your visualization practice. This makes the mental images more vivid and realistic.

Practice Consistently: Consistency is key to effective visualization. Practice daily to reinforce the mental pathways associated with your goals.

Stay Positive: Focus on positive outcomes and believe in your ability to achieve your goals. Positive thinking enhances the effectiveness of visualization.

2. Practice Gratitude Regularly:

Make gratitude a regular part of your life by incorporating simple practices that help you focus on the positive aspects of your life.

Strategies for Practicing Gratitude:

Keep a Gratitude Journal: Write down three things you are grateful for each day. Reflect on these entries regularly to reinforce positive thinking.

Express Gratitude to Others: Take time to thank the people in your life who have made a positive impact. Expressing gratitude strengthens relationships and fosters a positive environment.

Practice Gratitude Meditation: Spend a few minutes each day meditating on the things you are grateful for. Visualize these positive aspects and feel the gratitude in your heart.

Focus on the Present: Appreciate the present moment and the good things happening right now. Mindfulness and gratitude go hand in hand in enhancing your well-being.

Exercises to Harness the Power of Gratitude and Visualization

1. Create a Vision Board:

A vision board is a visual representation of your goals and dreams. Creating a vision board helps you to clarify your goals, visualize your desired outcomes, and stay motivated.

Steps to Create a Vision Board:

Gather Supplies: You will need a board (corkboard, poster board, or a large piece of paper), magazines, scissors, glue, and markers.

Reflect on Your Goals: Spend some time thinking about your long-term and short-term goals in different areas of your life, such as career, health, relationships, and personal growth.

Find Inspirational Images and Words: Look through magazines or print images from the internet that represent your goals and dreams. Choose pictures, words, and quotes that resonate with you.

Arrange and Glue: Arrange the images and words on your board in a way that feels meaningful and inspiring to you. Once you're happy with the layout, glue everything in place.

Display Your Vision Board: Place your vision board in a prominent location where you will see it daily. This could be your bedroom, office, or any other space where you spend a lot of time.

Example of a Vision Board:

Career: Images of a successful businessperson, a dream office, and the words "Leadership" and "Innovation."

Health: Pictures of healthy food, a person exercising, and the words "Wellness" and "Vitality."

Relationships: Photos of happy families and friends, and the words "Love" and "Connection."

Personal Growth: Images of books, a person meditating, and the words "Growth" and "Mindfulness."

2. Write Down Three Things You're Grateful for Each Day:

Keeping a gratitude journal is a simple yet powerful practice that helps you focus on the positive aspects of your life. By writing down three things you are grateful for each day, you can cultivate a positive mindset and enhance your well-being.

Steps for Keeping a Gratitude Journal:

Choose a Journal: Select a notebook or digital app to use as your gratitude journal.

Set Aside Time: Dedicate a specific time each day to write in your journal. Many people find it helpful to write in the morning or before bed.

Write Down Three Things: Each day, write down three things you are grateful for. These can be big or small, such as a kind gesture from a friend, a beautiful sunset, or a personal achievement.

Reflect and Review: Regularly review your gratitude journal entries. Reflect on the positive aspects of your life and the progress you have made.

Example of a Gratitude Journal Entry:

Date: [Date]

1. I am grateful for the support and encouragement of my family.

2. I am grateful for the opportunity to learn and grow in my career.

3. I am grateful for the beautiful weather today, which allowed me to enjoy a walk in the park.

The Importance of Gratitude and Visualization

Practicing gratitude and visualization can have a profound impact on your overall well-being and success. Here's why these practices are so important:

1. Enhances Positive Thinking:

Gratitude and visualization help you focus on positive thoughts and experiences. This positive thinking can improve your mood, reduce stress, and increase your overall sense of happiness.

2. Boosts Motivation and Confidence:

Visualization helps you mentally rehearse your success, boosting your confidence and motivation. Gratitude reinforces your belief in your ability to achieve your goals by highlighting the positive aspects of your life.

3. Improves Mental and Emotional Health:

Both gratitude and visualization have been shown to improve mental and emotional health. Gratitude reduces symptoms of depression and anxiety, while visualization helps to reduce stress and enhance well-being.

4. Fosters Resilience:

Practicing gratitude and visualization can increase your resilience, helping you to cope with challenges and setbacks more effectively. These practices provide a sense of control and optimism, enabling you to bounce back from adversity.

5. Strengthens Relationships:

Expressing gratitude can strengthen your relationships by fostering positive interactions and building trust. Visualization can help you improve your social skills and interactions by mentally rehearsing positive outcomes.

Developing a Consistent Practice

Developing a consistent practice of gratitude and visualization involves making these practices a regular part of your daily routine. Here are some tips to help you develop and maintain these practices:

1. Set Specific Goals:

Set specific goals for your gratitude and visualization practices. For example, aim to write in your gratitude journal every day and visualize your goals for five minutes each morning.

2. Create a Routine:

Incorporate gratitude and visualization into your daily routine. Choose a specific time each day to practice, such as in the morning or before bed.

3. Use Reminders:

Set reminders to prompt you to practice gratitude and visualization. Use alarms, sticky notes, or digital notifications to help you stay on track.

4. Stay Committed:

Commit to your gratitude and visualization practices for at least 30 days. Consistency is key to forming new habits and experiencing the benefits.

5. Reflect on Your Progress:

Regularly reflect on your progress and the impact of these practices on your life. Consider how gratitude and visualization have improved your mindset, motivation, and overall well-being.

Exercises to Deepen Your Practice

1. Gratitude Letter:

Writing a gratitude letter involves expressing your appreciation to someone who has made a positive impact on your life. This exercise can strengthen your relationship and enhance your sense of gratitude.

Steps for Writing a Gratitude Letter:

Choose a Recipient: Think of someone who has made a significant positive impact on your life. This could be a friend, family member, mentor, or colleague.

Write the Letter: Write a heartfelt letter expressing your gratitude. Be specific about what they did and how it positively affected you.

Deliver the Letter: If possible, deliver the letter in person and read it aloud to the recipient. If not, send it by mail or email.

Example of a Gratitude Letter:

Dear [Recipient's Name],

I hope this letter finds you well. I wanted to take a moment to express my heartfelt gratitude for the positive impact you have had on my life. Your support, kindness, and encouragement have meant the world to me.

Specifically, I am grateful for [specific action or support they provided]. This made a significant difference in my life by [explain how it affected you positively]. Your presence and support have helped me grow and achieve my goals, and for that, I am truly thankful.

Thank you for being such an incredible [friend, mentor, colleague]. I am so grateful to have you in my life.

With sincere appreciation,

[Your Name]

2. Guided Visualization Meditation:

Guided visualization meditation involves following a recorded meditation that guides you through a visualization exercise. This practice can help you deepen your visualization skills and enhance your focus.

Steps for Guided Visualization Meditation:

Find a Quiet Space: Choose a quiet and comfortable space where you can sit or lie down without distractions.

Choose a Guided Meditation: Find a guided visualization meditation that aligns with your goals. There are many available online or through meditation apps.

Follow the Guidance: Listen to the guided meditation and follow the instructions. Focus on creating vivid mental images and engaging all your senses.

Reflect on the Experience: After the meditation, take a few moments to reflect on the experience. Consider how it made you feel and any insights you gained.

Example of a Guided Visualization Meditation:

There are many guided visualization meditations available online. Here's a brief example script to get you started:

**Close your eyes and take a few deep breaths. As you breathe in, feel the air filling your lungs and energizing your body. As you breathe out, release any tension and let your body relax.

Now, imagine yourself in a peaceful and beautiful place. This could be a beach, a forest, or any place that feels calming and serene to you. Visualize the sights, sounds, and smells of this place. Feel the warmth of the sun on your skin, the gentle breeze, and the soothing sounds of nature.

In this peaceful place, visualize your goals and dreams. See yourself achieving these goals with confidence and ease. Imagine the steps you are taking to reach your goals and the positive outcomes you are experiencing. Feel the emotions of joy, satisfaction, and fulfilment as you achieve your dreams.

Take a few moments to fully immerse yourself in this visualization. When you are ready, slowly bring your awareness back to the present moment. Open your eyes and take a deep breath, feeling refreshed and motivated. **

Inspirational Quotes

Inspirational quotes can serve as powerful reminders of the importance of practicing gratitude and visualization. Here are a few quotes to inspire you:

"Gratitude turns what we have into enough." – Anonymous

"The more you praise and celebrate your life, the more there is in life to celebrate." – Oprah Winfrey

"What you think, you become. What you feel, you attract. What you imagine, you create." – Buddha

"Gratitude is not only the greatest of virtues but the parent of all others." – Cicero

"Visualization is daydreaming with a purpose." – Bo Bennett

Conclusion

Gratitude and visualization are powerful practices that can enhance your success, well-being, and overall quality of life. By focusing on the positive aspects of your life and mentally rehearsing your desired outcomes, you can cultivate a positive mindset, increase your motivation, and improve your ability to achieve your goals.

The stories of individuals like Jim Carrey, Oprah Winfrey, and Michael Phelps demonstrate the transformative power of gratitude and visualization. Their successes highlight the importance of believing in your dreams, being grateful for what you have, and visualizing your desired outcomes.

Incorporating gratitude and visualization into your daily routine involves setting specific goals, creating a consistent practice, and using exercises to deepen your practice. By making these practices a regular part of your life, you can unlock their full potential and create a fulfilling and successful life.

Chapter 10: Maintain Balance and Well-being

Overview

Achieving success in life is not solely about working hard or striving relentlessly toward your goals. It also involves maintaining a balanced lifestyle and prioritizing your overall well-being. Health and happiness are integral to sustained success, as they ensure you have the energy, resilience, and mental clarity needed to pursue your aspirations effectively. Neglecting your well-being can lead to burnout, stress, and diminished productivity, undermining your long-term success.

This chapter delves into the importance of balance and well-being, showcasing real-life examples of successful individuals who prioritize their health and happiness. It offers practical tips for maintaining a balanced lifestyle and guides you through exercises to integrate self-care, mindfulness, and stress management into your routine. By understanding and implementing these principles, you can enhance your overall quality of life and achieve lasting success.

The Importance of Balance and Well-being

Maintaining balance and well-being involves taking a holistic approach to your life, ensuring that you allocate time and energy to various aspects, including work, health, relationships, and personal growth. A balanced lifestyle promotes physical, emotional, and mental health, enabling you to function at your best.

Benefits of Maintaining Balance and Well-being:

Enhanced Productivity: Regular self-care and downtime can boost your productivity by preventing burnout and ensuring you have the energy to perform effectively.

Improved Mental Health: Prioritizing well-being can reduce stress, anxiety, and depression, leading to better mental health and emotional resilience.

Better Physical Health: Incorporating regular exercise, a balanced diet, and sufficient sleep into your routine can improve your physical health and longevity.

Stronger Relationships: A balanced lifestyle allows you to nurture your relationships, fostering deeper connections and support systems.

Increased Happiness: Taking time for activities that bring you joy and fulfilment enhances your overall happiness and life satisfaction.

Real-Life Examples

1. Arianna Huffington:

Arianna Huffington, the co-founder of The Huffington Post and founder of Thrive Global, is a strong advocate for the importance of sleep and well-being. After collapsing from exhaustion in 2007, Huffington realized the critical need for balance in her life. This experience led her to prioritize sleep, self-care, and stress management.

Through her work at Thrive Global, Huffington promotes the idea that well-being is essential for productivity and success. She encourages individuals and organizations to prioritize health and happiness, offering resources and tools to help people lead more balanced lives. Huffington's journey highlights the transformative power of prioritizing well-being and the positive impact it can have on personal and professional success.

2. Richard Branson:

Richard Branson, the founder of the Virgin Group, emphasizes the importance of work-life balance as a key to his productivity and happiness. Branson believes that taking time for relaxation, exercise, and hobbies is crucial for maintaining high levels of creativity and energy.

Branson practices what he preaches by incorporating activities such as kite surfing, playing tennis, and spending time with family into his daily routine. He encourages his employees to prioritize their well-being, fostering a company culture that values balance and happiness. Branson's approach demonstrates that achieving success does not require sacrificing personal well-being and that balance is integral to long-term productivity and satisfaction.

Tips for Maintaining Balance and Well-being

1. Schedule Regular Downtime and Self-Care Activities:

Incorporate regular breaks and self-care activities into your schedule to ensure you have time to recharge and relax. Downtime is essential for preventing burnout and maintaining overall well-being.

Strategies for Scheduling Downtime:

Set Boundaries: Establish clear boundaries between work and personal time. Avoid overworking and ensure you have time for relaxation and leisure.

Plan Breaks: Schedule short breaks throughout your workday to rest and recharge. Use this time to stretch, take a walk, or practice deep breathing.

Prioritize Self-Care: Allocate time for self-care activities such as exercise, hobbies, and spending time with loved ones. Make these activities a non-negotiable part of your routine.

2. Practice Mindfulness and Stress Management Techniques:

Mindfulness and stress management techniques can help you stay grounded, reduce stress, and improve your overall well-being. These practices enhance your ability to cope with challenges and maintain a positive mindset.

Strategies for Practicing Mindfulness:

Meditation: Incorporate a daily meditation practice to calm your mind and reduce stress. Start with just a few minutes each day and gradually increase the duration.

Mindful Breathing: Practice mindful breathing exercises to center yourself and manage stress. Focus on your breath, taking slow, deep inhales and exhales.

Body Scan: Perform a body scan meditation to bring awareness to different parts of your body, releasing tension and promoting relaxation.

3. Maintain a Healthy Lifestyle:

A healthy lifestyle is foundational to overall well-being. Prioritize physical health through regular exercise, a balanced diet, and sufficient sleep.

Strategies for Maintaining a Healthy Lifestyle:

Exercise Regularly: Aim for at least 30 minutes of physical activity most days of the week. Choose activities you enjoy to make exercise a sustainable part of your routine.

Eat a Balanced Diet: Focus on a diet rich in fruits, vegetables, whole grains, lean proteins, and healthy fats. Avoid excessive consumption of processed foods, sugar, and alcohol.

Prioritize Sleep: Ensure you get 7-9 hours of quality sleep each night. Establish a consistent sleep schedule and create a relaxing bedtime routine to promote restful sleep.

4. Foster Strong Relationships:

Building and maintaining strong relationships is essential for emotional support and overall happiness. Invest time and effort into nurturing your connections with family, friends, and colleagues.

Strategies for Fostering Relationships:

Communicate Regularly: Stay in touch with loved ones through regular phone calls, video chats, or in-person visits. Communication strengthens bonds and fosters a sense of connection.

Show Appreciation: Express gratitude and appreciation for the people in your life. Small gestures of kindness and acknowledgment can go a long way in strengthening relationships.

Participate in Social Activities: Engage in social activities and events to build new relationships and strengthen existing ones. Join clubs, organizations, or community groups that align with your interests.

5. Pursue Personal Growth and Hobbies:

Engaging in activities that promote personal growth and fulfilment enhances your overall well-being. Pursue hobbies and interests that bring you joy and satisfaction.

Strategies for Pursuing Personal Growth:

Set Personal Goals: Identify areas for personal growth and set specific, achievable goals. This could include learning a new skill, taking up a hobby, or pursuing further education.

Make Time for Hobbies: Allocate time for activities you enjoy, whether it's reading, painting, playing a musical instrument, or gardening. Hobbies provide a creative outlet and promote relaxation.

Seek New Experiences: Embrace new experiences and challenges that contribute to your personal growth. Travel, take on new projects, or explore different cultures and perspectives.

Exercises to Maintain Balance and Well-being

1. Weekly Schedule Exercise:

Planning your week to include time for work, exercise, relaxation, and hobbies helps you maintain a balanced lifestyle. This exercise encourages you to create a structured schedule that prioritizes well-being.

Steps for Creating a Weekly Schedule:

Identify Priorities: Determine your top priorities for the week, including work tasks, exercise, relaxation, and hobbies.

Allocate Time Blocks: Allocate specific time blocks for each priority. Ensure you have time for all aspects of your life, including self-care and leisure activities.

Set Boundaries: Establish clear boundaries for work and personal time. Avoid overcommitting and ensure you have time to rest and recharge.

Review and Adjust: At the end of the week, review your schedule and make adjustments as needed. Reflect on what worked well and what could be improved.

Example of a Weekly Schedule:

Monday:

7:00 AM - 8:00 AM: Exercise (Yoga)

9:00 AM - 12:00 PM: Work (Meetings and Project Work)

12:00 PM - 1:00 PM: Lunch Break

1:00 PM - 5:00 PM: Work (Emails and Administrative Tasks)

5:00 PM - 6:00 PM: Relaxation (Reading)

6:00 PM - 7:00 PM: Dinner

7:00 PM - 8:00 PM: Hobby (Painting)

Tuesday:

7:00 AM - 8:00 AM: Exercise (Jogging)

9:00 AM - 12:00 PM: Work (Client Meetings)

12:00 PM - 1:00 PM: Lunch Break

1:00 PM - 5:00 PM: Work (Project Development)

5:00 PM - 6:00 PM: Relaxation (Meditation)

6:00 PM - 7:00 PM: Dinner

7:00 PM - 8:00 PM: Social Activity (Virtual Hangout with Friends)

2. Mindfulness Practice Exercise:

Incorporating a daily mindfulness or meditation practice can help you reduce stress and improve your overall well-being. This exercise guides you through a simple mindfulness practice.

Steps for Mindfulness Practice:

Find a Quiet Space: Choose a quiet and comfortable space where you can sit or lie down without distractions.

Set a Timer: Set a timer for your mindfulness practice. Start with just 5-10 minutes and gradually increase the duration as you become more comfortable.

Focus on Your Breath: Close your eyes and take a few deep breaths. Focus on the sensation of your breath as you inhale and exhale. Notice the rise and fall of your chest or abdomen.

Observe Your Thoughts: As you focus on your breath, you may notice thoughts arising. Simply observe these thoughts without judgment and gently bring your attention back to your breath.

Practice Regularly: Aim to practice mindfulness daily. Consistency is key to experiencing the benefits of mindfulness.

Example of a Mindfulness Practice:

Mindful Breathing Exercise:

Sit comfortably with your back straight and your hands resting on your lap. Close your eyes and take a deep breath in through your nose, feeling your lungs expand.

Exhale slowly through your mouth, releasing any tension in your body.

Continue to breathe deeply and naturally, focusing on the sensation of your breath. Notice the cool air entering your nostrils and the warm air leaving your mouth.

If your mind wanders, gently bring your attention back to your breath.

After a few minutes, slowly open your eyes and take a moment to notice how you feel.

The Importance of Balance and Well-being for Sustained Success

Maintaining balance and well-being is essential for sustained success and overall quality of life. Here's why these principles are so important:

1. Prevents Burnout:

Regular self-care and downtime prevent burnout by allowing you to recharge and relax. Burnout can lead to decreased productivity, increased stress, and a negative impact on your physical and mental health.

2. Enhances Productivity:

A balanced lifestyle enhances productivity by ensuring you have the energy and focus needed to perform effectively. Regular breaks and self-care activities boost your creativity and problem-solving skills.

3. Improves Mental and Emotional Health:

Prioritizing well-being reduces stress, anxiety, and depression, leading to better mental and emotional health. A positive mindset and emotional resilience contribute to overall happiness and life satisfaction.

4. Supports Physical Health:

Incorporating regular exercise, a balanced diet, and sufficient sleep into your routine supports physical health and longevity. Good physical health is foundational to overall well-being.

5. Fosters Strong Relationships:

A balanced lifestyle allows you to nurture your relationships, fostering deeper connections and support systems. Strong relationships provide emotional support and contribute to overall happiness.

6. Promotes Personal Growth:

Engaging in activities that promote personal growth and fulfilment enhances your overall well-being. Pursuing hobbies and interests that bring you joy contributes to a sense of purpose and satisfaction.

Inspirational Quotes

Inspirational quotes can serve as powerful reminders of the importance of maintaining balance and well-being. Here are a few quotes to inspire you:

"Take care of your body. It's the only place you have to live." – Jim Rohn

"Balance is not something you find, it's something you create." – Jana Kingsford

"Happiness is not a matter of intensity but of balance, order, rhythm, and harmony." – Thomas Merton

"Self-care is how you take your power back." – Lalah Delia

"You can't pour from an empty cup. Take care of yourself first." – Anonymous

Conclusion

Achieving success in life is not solely about working hard or striving relentlessly toward your goals. It also involves maintaining a balanced lifestyle and prioritizing your overall well-being. Health and happiness are integral to sustained success, as they ensure you have the energy, resilience, and mental clarity needed to pursue your aspirations effectively.

The stories of individuals like Arianna Huffington and Richard Branson demonstrate the transformative power of prioritizing well-being and the positive impact it can have on personal and professional success. Their successes highlight the importance of balance and self-care in achieving lasting success.

Incorporating balance and well-being into your daily routine involves setting specific goals, creating a structured schedule, and using exercises to integrate self-care, mindfulness, and stress management into your life. By making these practices a regular part of your life, you can enhance your overall quality of life and achieve sustained success.

Remember, maintaining balance and well-being is an ongoing process that requires intentional effort and a commitment to self-care. By prioritizing your health and happiness, you can create a fulfilling and successful life that supports your long-term goals and aspirations.

The Path to Success: Principles for Personal and Professional Growth

About the Author

Dr. Kumar Abhisek is a seasoned pharmaceutical professional with over 24 years of experience in the industry. He holds a Bachelor's degree in Pharmacy, a Postgraduate Certificate in Sales and Marketing from IIM-Kozhikode, and honorary doctorates from Thames International University and Hassen International University. Known for his innovative approach to brand management and his commitment to personal growth, Dr Abhisek has successfully launched and managed key pharmaceutical brands, earning numerous accolades throughout his career. He is also a certified hypnotherapist and a dedicated advocate for holistic wellness, blending his professional expertise with a passion for empowering others to achieve their full potential.